Concise guides
to planning

Healthy Cities? Design for Well-being

Healthy Cities? Design for Well-being

Tim Townshend

LUND
HUMPHRIES

First published in 2022 by Lund Humphries

Lund Humphries
Office 3, Book House
261A City Road
London EC1V 1JX
UK

www.lundhumphries.com

Healthy Cities? Design for Well-being
© Tim Townshend, 2022
All rights reserved

ISBN (hardback): 978–1–84822–330–1
ISBN (eBook Mobi): 978–1–84822–332–5
ISBN (eBook ePub): 978–1–84822–331–8
ISBN (eBook PDF): 978–1–84822–329–5

Concise Guides to Planning (Print): ISSN 2516–8177
Concise Guides to Planning (Online): ISSN 2516–8185

A Cataloguing-in-Publication record for this book is
available from the British Library.

Cover design by Stefi Orazi

Copy edited by Pamela Bertram
Typeset by Jacqui Cornish
Proofread by Patrick Cole
Set in Favorit
Printed in the United Kingdom

All illustrations and photographs are the author's own with the exception of the following
figures: Fig.1.2 T. Arnadottir (2020); Fig.1.8 Wikimedia Commons; Fig.2.1 Roser, Ortiz-Espina
and Ritchie (2013, revised 2019); Fig.2.2 ONS (2020); Fig.2.3 Dahlgren and Whitehead (1991);
Fig.2.4 Barton and Grant (2006); Fig.4.3 Peter Landers; Fig.4.6 Adapted from Royal Society for
Public Health, 'Health on the High Street: Running on Empty 2018'; Fig.5.3 Redrawing by
Thomas Bohm, User Design, Illustration and Typesetting, from author's illustration; Fig.6.2
Photo by kind permission of Haley Walton, Architect; Fig.6.5 Graph redrawing by Thomas Bohm,
User Design, Illustration and Typesetting, from author's illustration; Fig.7.1 New West End
Company; Fig.7.2 Presseye, Belfast; Fig.7.4 Nationwide Building Society; Fig.7.5 Karakusevic
Carson Architects; Fig.7.6 U+I.

Contents

Foreword

I really enjoyed reading this incredibly powerful and insightful book. In many ways it carves out a unique and incredibly timely agenda for putting health and well-being back at the heart of planning and urban design. But it does much more than this – it provides a detailed case for why healthcare providers and public health officials need to engage with planning and urban design issues if we are truly to make a paradigm shift towards community-level preventative approaches to healthcare.

What truly inspired me about this book was the rich detail involved across each chapter that provided new nuggets of information and fresh insights even into areas of planning that I thought I knew well, such as the context-setting introductory chapter. It helps, too, that the book is so well written, its arguments clearly set out and the case convincingly made for why each of the issues introduced in successive chapters deserves to be taken seriously by practitioners of planning and public health officials. Over the course of the book a clear intellectual agenda emerges for putting health and well-being at the centre of how we create better, healthier, more enjoyable cities for the future.

I cannot recommend this book to you highly enough. I hope you enjoy reading it and gain as much from it as I certainly did. It is also a wonderful companion to some of the other books in this *Concise Guides to Planning* series, including *Planning, Sustainability and Nature* (Dave Counsell and Rob Stoneman), *Green Infrastructure Planning* (Ian Mell), *Planning, Transport and Accessibility* (Carey Curtis), *Conserving the Historic Environment* (John Pendlebury and Jules Brown), *The Urban Design Process* (Philip Black and Taki Eddin Sonbli), *Planning for an Ageing Society* (Rose Gilroy) and *Children and Planning* (Claire Freeman and Andrea Cook).

Graham Haughton, Series Editor

Acknowledgements

I would like to thank the following people for agreeing to be interviewed in connection with this volume: Caroline Clapson – Planning Consultant; Gillian Dick – Spatial Planning Manager, Glasgow City Council; Martin Evans – Creative Director, U+I Plc; Tom Gray – Senior Ecologist, ARUP; Paul Karakusevic – Founding Partner, Karakusevic Carson Architects; Jess Kennedy – Associate Director, ARUP; Katherine Quigley – Social Investment Manager, Nationwide Building Society; Rosie Rowe – Programme Director, Healthy Bicester; Dhruv Sookoo – Architect, MetWork; Zoe Webb – Senior Environmental Consultant, ARUP. Apologies to anyone I have missed.

Special thanks to Liz Brooks for her invaluable assistance with proofreading and copy editing.

Chapter 1   **Lessons from History:**
                     Special Places to Everyday Spaces

In this chapter, we trace 2,500 years of human history, from ancient Greece to the end of modernist-inspired planning in the late 20th century, and reflect on key themes that run through this period.

Early beginnings

The notion that certain places are infused with special properties that are good for health is a very ancient one and transcends cultures across the globe. From the 5th century BCE onwards, for example, the Greeks built an entire city dedicated to healing – Epidaurus, in the eastern Peloponnese. It was built over many generations and at its height, Epidaurus could house several thousand visitors recovering from illness. People travelled from all over Greece to visit the city, though of course this would only have been an option for the relatively wealthy.

The natural landscape was very much integral to the original city, and Epidaurus was sometimes referred to as the 'sacred grove' because the buildings were surrounded by trees (Alt, 2017). The city contained a variety of buildings, including temples where ritualistic purification and healing were performed. However, many structures were secular, designed for exercise and entertainment (Fig.1.1). As embodied by the city, the healing process for the ancient Greeks included mental, spiritual and physical (bodily) needs.

↑
Figure 1.1
The amphitheatre at Epidaurus, built for entertainment and mental stimulation,
showing the relationship to the landscape beyond

Water and healing

Spas

A key part of the curative processes at Epidaurus involved
washing and cleansing. Water, of course, is the most essential
element of life and humans can only survive a few days without
it. Over millennia, our relationship with water has also been
multifaceted. Used as a source of food and for transportation,
it has also been a source of spiritual inspiration. To the ancient
Greeks and Romans, sources of water, such as springs and
rivers, had their own distinctive deities. Even today, most major
religions include water-based ceremonies as part of ritualistic
purification.

In Europe, the notion of the healing properties of water
was developed by the Romans, who believed that different

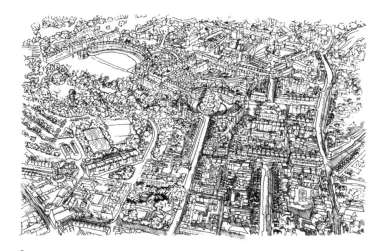

↑
Figure 1.2
A bird's-eye view of Bath – an embodiment of 18th-century ideas of healthiness

temperatures and mineral content could be utilised in different cures. For example, sulphur springs were believed to relieve muscle weakness, while alkaline springs were recommended for tuberculosis (Jackson, 1990). In the 1st century CE, during the Roman occupation of Britain, the Romans developed an extensive water-based spa at Bath, Somerset, based on a much more ancient sacred Celtic site (Cunliffe, 1984). This flourished until the Romans left Britain (around 410 CE) when Bath was partly abandoned and knowledge pertaining to the curative properties of water was lost. However, during the Italian Renaissance in the 15th century, water cures again began to be taken seriously, although it took another 200 years for physicians in England to embrace this knowledge. It was during the Georgian period, therefore, that taking the waters at Bath once more became a fashionable cure for a range of ailments.

Bath's prosperity was driven by a serendipitous coming together of then contemporary medical advice; wealth, provided by Ralph Allen who owned local limestone quarries; fashion, provided by Beau Nash, a celebrated 'dandy' associated with the city; and architecture, designed by John Wood the Elder. Wealthy visitors flocked to the city, not just to take the waters, but to go to the theatre, socialise and gamble. The city therefore catered for visitors' physical, mental and social needs, rather like a Georgian version of Epidaurus.

Symbolic reference to health, however, was also embedded in the very physicality of the city. The architectural set pieces of Bath – Queen Square, The Circus and The Royal Crescent (Fig.1.2) – are a masterclass in order, proportion and, importantly, harmony between buildings and planting/landscape. This balance was thought to reflect that of the cosmos and was deemed essential for physical and mental health to flourish.

Coastal resorts

Tuberculosis – commonly called 'consumption' – was the number one killer of Britons for most of the 19th century and there was no cure. Medical opinion at the time was that such diseases were transmitted by 'miasma' – foul-smelling air that built up in the narrow courts and alleys in cities. Doctors suggested that consumptives needed air that was fresh and well circulated, and seaside resorts were a preferred source (Morris, 2018).

Sea bathing also became increasingly popular from the mid-18th century onwards. Again, this was encouraged by prominent physicians, who recommended both submersion in, and drinking of, seawater and proclaimed that saltwater cures were superior to those provided by inland spas. These factors led to the growth of seaside towns such as Bournemouth, Torquay and Hastings, greatly assisted from the mid-19th century by the rapid expansion of the railway network.

—

Water and harm

> . . . we have then quite sufficient data to account for the surplus mortality . . . in consequence of the floods from the Aire which, it must be added, like all other rivers in the service

of manufacture, flows into the city at one end clear and transparent, and flows out at the other end thick, black, and foul, smelling of all possible refuse.

Engels ([1845]1987)

The story of water and health is not, however, an entirely positive one. During the industrial revolution in Britain there was a dramatic change. Many industrial processes required vast amounts of water, and waterways were also used to transport goods. The river- and canal-sides of major cities became lined with warehouses, mills and works. Industries such as textile manufacture and tanneries poured vast quantities of noxious, unwanted chemicals straight into the river system, where they mixed with human and animal waste. As there was little control over the flow of water, houses near the banks were often inundated with the poisonous content of the watercourse. As a result, and as observed by Engels, rivers were basically open sewers and implicated in the high rates of mortality of those who lived near them.

Consequently, in the 19th century only the most desperate would live next to most urban watercourses, though working people generally had little choice about where they lived. The rapid urbanisation that occurred in 19th-century industrial towns and cities led to appalling housing conditions which facilitated the spread of deadly diseases such as cholera. However, this was also a period of laissez-faire economics, and state intervention was regarded as highly suspicious by the powerful in society. Therefore, for several decades, there was little official response.

Gradually, however, there was an increasing recognition that the situation could not go on. In 1832 a major cholera outbreak killed large numbers of people and the concept of 'public health' gained momentum. In 1840, the British government set up a parliamentary committee to report on the health of towns. This was the beginning of a series of official reports, as well as treatises written from a philosophical, or political, stance (Engels, [1845]1987). One of the most significant was Edwin Chadwick's report on the sanitary conditions of the working classes (Chadwick, [1842]2012). This revealed, for example, that the average life expectancy of a labourer in Liverpool was a truly appalling 15 years. Such compelling evidence could not go on being ignored.

——

The origins of public health

There were further cholera outbreaks in 1848–9 and 1853–4, and while miasma theory continued to hold sway, a Dr John Snow, based in Soho, London, mapped cholera cases, proving that the disease was spread by contaminated water. However, while understanding of both the problems and consequences was increasing, very little changed. Inertia in the system and a resistance to state regulation prevented action. While in 1868 the Torrens Act allowed local authorities to demolish unfit dwellings, there was no mechanism for replacement, and in some cases, this made the situation worse by increasing overcrowding in the remaining housing stock.

It was not until 1875 that the first effective legislation was introduced, in the form of the Second Public Health Act, which compelled local authorities to act. It consolidated previous sanitation legislation and required urban authorities to make byelaws for new housing, to ensure structural stability, provide effective drainage and air circulation, and establish that all houses have their own toilet. In effect it was the first urban planning act, though it was not labelled as such, and while it produced housing that was often somewhat monotonous in design, it contributed significantly to improvements in the health and life expectancy of working people.

Given the incredibly unhealthy situations found in cities, the question often arises as to whether people were forced out of the countryside into cities, or did they leave voluntarily during industrialisation? Here we begin unpicking the culturally constructed urban versus countryside debate. Many British people today have a very romantic view of the countryside; however, the truth is that in the 19th century, rural living for most people meant grinding poverty. Yes, there may have been fresh air, but there was precious little else. Cities provided opportunities – for employment, for betterment and to meet new people, perhaps to find a life partner. In other words, people were responding to a basic urge to make the most of life. While it might seem counter-intuitive to express this in terms of modern concepts of 'well-being', that desire of people to reach their potential can be included in the concept, as discussed early in Chapter 2 and in later discussions in this volume.

Visionaries and paternalists

In parallel to the development of the public health movement, there were series of experimental, or 'model', projects, which together underpin a British contribution to urban planning/design that is still influential today. Full and detailed accounts of their development are available elsewhere (see the further reading list at the end of this chapter), so what is contained below is intended as a brief summary and basis for further exploration.

New Lanark

The first water-powered mills of the industrial revolution were located in relatively rural locations and needed to attract workers. New Lanark was of this type. Established in the 1780s on the River Clyde, it was situated 25 miles south-east of Glasgow. Although initially established by David Dale, it is with his son-in-law, Robert Owen – who took over as manager, and subsequently became owner – that New Lanark is most associated.

Owen was a social reformer. His philosophy, which is still readily available and worth reading (Owen, [1813]1991), was founded on the belief that people were largely a product of their environment and that their behaviour would only improve when their surroundings did.[1] Today this would be labelled as 'environmental determinism' and regarded as highly questionable. However, given that he was writing over 200 years ago, when the living conditions of working people were appalling, it is difficult not to be sympathetic with Owen's opinion.

Owen aimed to improve the health and wellbeing of his workers by, for example, introducing cleanliness regimes inside and outside the home. Kitchen gardens provided a reliable source of wholesome fresh produce, and workers were attended by a doctor when ill. Moreover, everyone had access to an education, which was of a remarkable standard for the time. He even wrote about the need to cultivate habits in children that would contribute to 'happiness' in later life, for the benefit of the individual and the community (Owen, [1813]1991). He therefore addressed physical, social and psychological issues which might be related to the more contemporary concepts of health and well-being examined in Chapter 2.

In terms of built form, the buildings of New Lanark are robustly constructed from local sandstone, with slate roofs. They have simple and dignified forms, though there is a nod to classicism in later structures. Overall, the buildings create a harmonious and unpretentious whole and are a physical embodiment of Owen's egalitarian ideas (Fig.1.3).

↑
Figure 1.3
New Lanark, No. 1 Mill (from Robert Owen's House)

Although to modern eyes this initiative might seem paternalistic, or even 'totalitarian', in its attempts to shape workers' behaviour, in its time, New Lanark was viewed as both socially and economically successful. Owen was inspired to try and repeat this success in America so he purchased 30,000 acres of land in Indiana in 1825 and named it New Harmony. The project, though apparently a well-ordered community, did not thrive, however, and Owen soon withdrew. Importantly, the industrialising world had moved on. Water power had largely given way to steam and the idea of industrial 'villages', of whatever form and/or governance, was already looking anachronistic. In short, they were never going to compete with the might of the rapidly expanding industrial cities of the following period.

Saltaire

Saltaire, West Yorkshire, was built from 1851 onwards and was the largest of the industrial model villages of the mid-19th century. Unlike Owen, however, the founder Titus Salt wrote almost nothing of his motivations for building Saltaire and it is necessary to make deductions from the physical evidence of the village itself and a few remaining records of his business practice. We do know that unlike Owen, who regarded religion as a barrier to progress, Salt was a member of the Congregationalist Church, a branch of Protestantism that specifically promoted the ideas of 'self-improvement' for working people in the 19th century.

That ideal of self-improvement is clear in Saltaire – for example, the Working Men's Institute offering 'wholesome activities' in a lecture hall, reading room, library, billiards room and gymnasium, which were considered facilities for the improvement of mind and body. No public houses were allowed in the village, although there is no evidence that Salt was part of the temperance movement.[2] After the village was complete, Salt also provided Robert's Park – a large, open area for fresh air and recreation, and land for allotment gardens to grow fresh produce.

Salt was an extremely shrewd businessman. He made his fortune by seizing opportunities that others missed. Before moving to what was the greenfield site of Saltaire, he owned several mills in Bradford which, in the 1840s, was an exceedingly unhealthy place. Salt clearly realised that a greenfield site would be much healthier for his workforce; and a healthier workforce was therefore likely to be a more productive one!

It would certainly be wrong to imagine that Saltaire was a kind of utopia for the mill workers who lived there, and life would still have been extremely tough by modern standards. While children received a basic education, they still went to work at nine years old, and workers were not paid any more generously than those employed by Salt's competitors. In the early 1980s, when I worked on a 'town scheme' to repair/restore the village (Fig.1.4), some of the residents retained memories stretching back many decades. I still have notebooks that contain observations from many of the people I met – for example, this recollection from Ida T. (then in her eighties) who had lived in the village all her life:

> It was especially hard for the women . . . We lived in a house on Mary Street. It was impossible to keep anything clean. The houses were lit by dirty gas mantels and the roads were unmade. Every time you put your washing out it would get covered in smuts and you'd have to start again . . . Many of the men were drinkers. After their shift they would head straight to the pubs on the Bradford Road and stayed there until their wives went and hauled them out for their supper.

Ida's memories of domestic drudgery, though referring to the 1920/30s, would have been familiar to those living in the village in the previous century. Her comments on the men's drinking showed that Salt had been astute in banning drinking establishments from the village, though by the 1900s the neighbouring borough of Shipley had expanded so that pubs were then situated within walking distance.

In focus: Saltaire housing

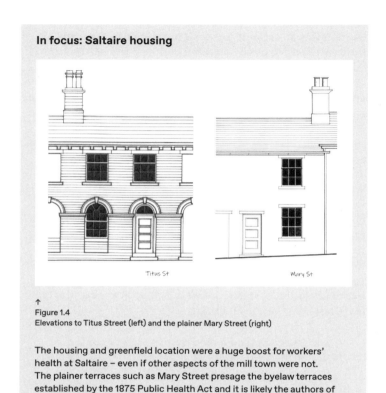

↑
Figure 1.4
Elevations to Titus Street (left) and the plainer Mary Street (right)

The housing and greenfield location were a huge boost for workers' health at Saltaire – even if other aspects of the mill town were not. The plainer terraces such as Mary Street presage the byelaw terraces established by the 1875 Public Health Act and it is likely the authors of the 1875 Act would have had Saltaire in mind as a well-known model of housing reform when they wrote the legislation.

Saltaire is designed as an architectural set piece. The gigantic mill – which was, when built, reputedly the world's largest industrial building – looms over the village. There was also a strict hierarchy of housing, which was supposed to reflect the position of workers in the factory, with the best houses on Albert Road intended for managerial staff. Although evidence suggests this regimented social manipulation never worked, for all the positives about the village, it is easy to imagine an atmosphere of stultifying control.

Bournville

Bournville was established some 40 years later (1893 onwards), on the outskirts of Birmingham, by cocoa manufacturer George Cadbury and is a leap forward in terms of the quality of the dwellings for working-class occupants (Fig.1.5).

A key element of Bournville is that Cadbury wanted to demonstrate that a temperate,[3] well-planned town could provide investors with a reasonable return (Cherry, 1996; Darley, 2007). Occupancy of the houses was not confined to workers in the factory, and they were rented out on the open market. Of significance to the theme of healthy environments, Bournville makes two interesting contributions. Firstly, the greenness of the environment: while houses vary in size, even the most modest properties have garden plots, and there are also allotments for growing plentiful fresh fruit and vegetables. The other key aspect was the inclusion of sports and recreation (Fig.1.6).

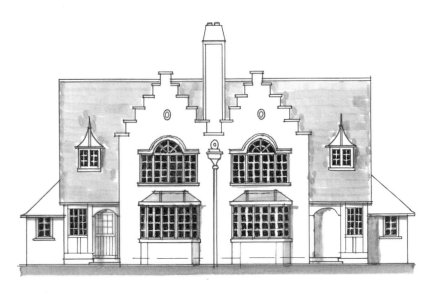

↑
Figure 1.5
A pair of Bournville cottages with decorative stepped gables

21

In focus: Bournville sports and recreation

↑
Figure 1.6   Sports pavilion, Bournville

Bournville had outstanding sports and recreation facilities to encourage healthy lifestyles from the outset, with the inclusion of a men's sports ground and a smaller women's recreation area. This separation and unequal provision may seem overtly sexist from a contemporary viewpoint, but this provision was remarkably progressive for the time. Men and women could exercise during lunch breaks, as well as in the evenings and at weekends.

By the 1920s the workforce of the factory had outgrown the sports facilities in the village and new facilities were provided a short distance away. By this time half of the Cadbury workforce was a member of at least one of the company athletic clubs. Also – reflecting a more enlightened age – there was no gender separation at the new grounds, and facilities included a lido for swimming and water sports. On a typical Saturday, up to 100 teams would play various sports involving up to 1,000 players (Chance, 2012). We return to the importance of providing opportunities for physical activity in Chapter 5, which highlights how ahead of its time the facilities at Bournville were.

Other developments

In terms of the development of model settlements, two that are particularly worthy of note are Port Sunlight and New Earswick. Port Sunlight was established by William Lever in 1888 on the Wirral Peninsula to house workers for the Lever Brothers soap factory. It was, therefore, contemporary with the development of Bournville. In its plan, it was more rigidly Beaux-Arts[4] than Bournville, with the Lady Lever Art Gallery providing a classical finale to the main south–north axis in the village (Fig.1.7).

The architecture of the housing takes inspiration from the vernacular English building tradition. Lever believed low-rise housing provided healthier dwellings than flats (Hubbard and Shippobottom, 2005), and the allotment gardens were also designed with health in mind. The execution of Port Sunlight does divide opinion, however. While some find the immaculate landscaping and decorative cottages delightful, to others the effect is over-regulated and contrived. It is a matter of personal taste, but while Port Sunlight is very green in nature, many of the landscaped spaces do appear decorative rather than useful.

↑
Figure 1.7
Lady Lever Art Gallery, Port Sunlight, the classical finale to the central axis

New Earswick, founded by Joseph Rowntree, the York chocolate manufacturer, in 1902, is also important. The village is a departure from previous experiments in that it was built well away from the Rowntree factory, so that the separation between place of work and residence is complete. Rowntree wanted the village to avoid associations of paternalism and 'charity', and that physical distance is a key element in this. Architects Barry Parker and Raymond Unwin were commissioned to design the first stages of the buildings, which are in a simple Arts and Crafts style. The houses all have gardens and were each provided with two fruit trees. Parker and Unwin are also of note because of their involvement with the garden city movement, outlined in the next section.

Unlike its predecessors, New Earswick is also not a static 'set piece': it has continued to be developed, with buildings added and redeveloped as needed. An interesting recent addition focusing on health and healthcare for older persons – New Lodge – is located next to the Folk Hall in the centre of the village.

Ebenezer Howard and garden cities

The establishment of the model industrial settlements of Bournville and Port Sunlight was contemporaneous with the early development of the garden city movement, associated with Ebenezer Howard. In 1888, Howard published *Tomorrow: A Peaceful Path to Real Reform*, later re-issued in a revised form and re-titled as *Garden Cities of To-morrow* in 1902 (and still in print) (Howard, 2009). Many commentators have pointed out that this more enticing title was undoubtedly key to its enduring appeal, although the original title reveals more of what was in Howard's mind.

Howard drew on a wide and eclectic mix of pre-existing theories, model settlements and even contemporary fiction for his inspiration. As such, some commentators have rather unfairly suggested that he was not an original thinker as his principal ideas all appear in earlier works. However, what was original was the way in which he drew them together (Hall, 2014). Themes

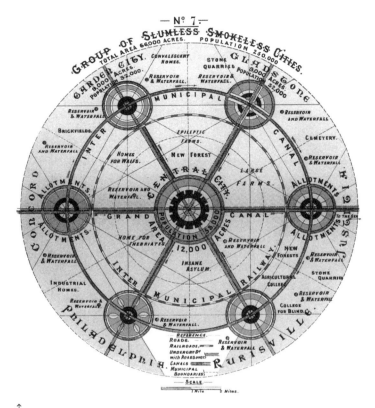

↑
Figure 1.8
Illustration of a group of 'smokeless slumless' cities, from
Garden Cities of To-morrow (Howard, 2009)

of integrating town and country, reform of capitalism, and the cooperative ownership and development of land were interwoven in his thinking. Howard posited that they could provide a vehicle that would deliver a fairer, more equal society.

Briefly, Howard advocated for a network of medium-sized, cooperatively developed settlements of some 32,000 inhabitants, built away from existing large cities and surrounded by green belts of mainly agricultural land (Fig.1.8). Combined, these would form conurbations with substantial populations, with each of the cities connected by a rapid transit system, allowing easy access between them. The settlements, he claimed, could therefore combine the social and economic advantages of the city, such as employment and cultural opportunities, with the health benefits – access to fresh air, space for recreation and healthy food – associated with the countryside.

Most of Howard's book is devoted to the social and development processes needed to create garden cities, rather than what they might look like, which was of much less interest to him. The basic mechanism was that land for garden cities would be purchased at what were then very depressed agricultural market values. The land would be bought and held in perpetuity by the community. As the new cities developed, the land values would rise and the increase in land value would be ploughed back into the community.

The Garden City Association was founded in 1899, and in 1903 the site of Letchworth Garden City was purchased. However, Howard's financial system was far too radical to work in Edwardian England. As a result, the scheme was chronically under-funded at the beginning and gradually Howard was edged out of financial decision-making.

Letchworth was designed by Parker and Unwin who, as already mentioned, were simultaneously working on New Earswick; their design also clearly owes much to earlier model settlements. The basic layout consists of tree-lined streets with Arts and Crafts cottages in generous garden plots (Fig.1.9). In many ways – unfortunately for Howard – it is this visual treatment that has become synonymous with English garden cities, rather than the revolutionary ideas for land and political reform that were his passion.

There are many useful accounts of Howard's work, some straightforward, others revisionist, which are worth consulting for further detail (Beevers, 1988; Hall, 2014). Today, 'garden villages' are enjoying government endorsement in England. In essence these are supposed to be 'mini' garden cities; however,

↑
Figure 1.9
Letchworth – a visual treatment that has become synonymous with garden cities

their definition is vague and their uptake has arguably been more to do with meeting pressing housing needs, rather than any radical intent (TCPA, 2017).

Patrick Geddes

Garden city concepts held sway in British planning theory for the first half of the 20th century. However, there were other important contributions in relation to health and well-being, particularly the work of Patrick Geddes. Geddes had a background in biology and in his early career travelled to Paris, where he encountered the work of Frédéric Le Play, an engineer who devoted his spare time to sociology and trying to improve the living conditions of the labouring classes.

In the 1880s, Geddes was working as a botanist in Edinburgh. He moved into the city's Old Town area, which at that time was approaching slum conditions, as he believed that to fully understand the problems facing those communities, he had to live among them. His life science roots are clear in his thinking. In the way that a doctor would diagnose an illness before treating it, Geddes promoted the idea of surveying and understanding urban problems, before planning, to ensure that plans would be based on adequate knowledge. This led him to propose 'conservative surgery' for cities: the painstaking renovation and improvement of slum areas, working with local communities, rather than imposing solutions on them (Geddes, 1949). His ideas of involving communities in their own solutions and conserving the historic fabric of the city were way ahead of their time and, sadly, largely ignored for several generations.

——

Health and modernism

Modernism in architecture/urban planning has antecedents in the 19th century when architects began to experiment with new materials and technologies, such as iron – and then steel – frames. Most buildings were dressed up in historical styles, but increasingly architects sought new forms of expression. The new 'clean' energy form of electricity, new technologies and mass production were inspirational. There was also an urgent desire for light and air to cast off the smoky gloom of the Victorian city.

However, the most radical experimentation was not in the UK, which clung on to the romanticism of the Arts and Crafts movement, but in the US and continental Europe. For example, in 1926/7 a housing exhibition at Weissenhof, Stuttgart, brought together key architects working in the new genre. This was a world away from the cosy cottages of Letchworth: the design was stripped back and unadorned, lean and fit, ready to take on the new age and clothed in hygienic white. As one of the key contributors to the Weissenhof exhibition, Charles Edouard Jeanneret (more commonly referred to by his pseudonym Le Corbusier) declared: houses were machines for living in (Le Corbusier, 2008) (Fig.1.10).

However, this was not to say that houses were intended to be detached from the natural world – quite the opposite. As the urban planner and historian Lewis Mumford observed, modern architecture did not want to imitate nature in applied decoration, as had been the case in previous centuries. Rather, the new architecture wanted to embrace nature, to provide the

↑
Figure 1.10
Le Corbusier, housing block, Weissenhof

ideal conditions for natural processes to take place. This was the 'biotechnical' world as Mumford saw it: 'What is a modern dwelling? The new home is primarily a biological institution; and the home is a specialised structure devoted to the functions of reproduction, nutrition and nurture' (Mumford, 1938, p.486).

This relationship between the natural world and buildings was intended to extend out from the individual home and to infuse the entire city. Buildings were to touch the earth lightly, to be built on stilts ('pilotis') so that the landscape would flow underneath, providing freedom and an uninterrupted opportunity for the activities of life to take place.

However, to make the whole city healthy and efficient, the modernists declared, it also had to be reconfigured. A year after the Stuttgart exhibition, the Congrès internationaux d'architecture moderne (CIAM), or International Congresses of Modern Architecture, was founded. Led by Le Corbusier, its most famous pronouncement on city planning came in the 1933 Charter of Athens. The Charter was divided into sections and outlined the functions of the city as dwelling, recreation, work and transportation. The chaotic industrial city did not satisfy the 'biological and physiological needs' of its inhabitants (CIAM, 1946). The solution was to zone the city according to its separate functions which would be connected through an efficient transportation system. The scale of the task, it declared, was monumental, but everything about the outcome should meet the needs of the community and the individual.

During the 1920s and 1930s there was little opportunity for the modernists to significantly influence urban planning. However, the devastation wrought by the Second World War (1939–45) meant that there was an acute shortage of housing across Europe and many cities required major reconstruction. In a war-ravaged world desperate not to repeat the mistakes of the past, modernist theories provided a beacon of hope.

Unfortunately, the optimism did not last. The health-promoting capacities of the new mass housing schemes as built in Britain were not realised. Cost-cutting and poor build quality meant that apartments might have been light and airy in fine weather but were often cold and damp during the British winter. Experimental heating and other services often did not work properly, and the landscaped grounds that were supposed to be shared by the community, and with nature, turned out to be windswept no-man's-lands, unloved and uncared for.

More fundamentally, the zoning of cities into different uses and designing them around the needs of the private car, rather than humans, was a monumental disaster. Urban motorways cutting noisy, polluted swathes through cities and communities, shut-down local services removing the cultural hub of neighbourhoods, and a host of other poor decisions, have left a legacy which – as will be examined in Chapter 3 – has clearly contributed to ill-health and lifestyle diseases, and today presents a monumental challenge.

There are many accounts of why modernism in planning was a failure, but from the perspective of this text, a key issue is that during the post-war period, 'health' simply stopped being a focus of what planning was trying to achieve, particularly as economies began to falter after the initial post-war boom. More broadly the whole concept of '*environmental determinism*' – the idea that people's lives could be transformed and improved primarily by intervention in the environment – became discredited, and urban planners and designers distanced themselves from those topics, including health, which had been associated with deterministic theories.

Conclusions

Trying to condense over 2,500 years of human history into a short chapter and then draw meaningful conclusions from that summary is clearly a challenge. However, looking back over key times and places, one cannot help being struck by the recurrent themes that run through that human experience.

1   *Nature*   Human relationship with 'nature'. From the sacred grove of Epidaurus, through to the landscaped set pieces of Georgian Bath, the garden city, or biotech modernism – the instinctive understanding that humans need to engage with a more natural world for physical and psychological health is clear and evident. This does not mean we all need to escape to the country – there is plenty of scope for nature in our cities, and this need is often entirely overlooked in modern development.

2   *Water*   Our relationship with water is a second theme. Water, for millennia, was revered for its spiritual and curative qualities. During the darkest periods of the industrial revolution that relationship was disregarded, and while today urban waterfronts have been effectively reclaimed and are now highly desirable, the therapeutic qualities of urban waterbodies are yet to be fully appreciated. Nevertheless, water remains an unpredictable element, and today the

consequences of flooding devastate the mental health of communities – a topic we return to in Chapter 5.

3 *Holistic health and well-being*   The final theme of the interplay between physical, mental and social health. Again, it was understood as far back as the establishment of Epidaurus that human health and well-being should be addressed holistically. This is as true for the many ailments that plagued the ancient world as for modern lifestyle diseases and we unpack this fully in Chapter 2.

___

Further reading

Cherry, G. (1996). *Town Planning in Britain since 1900: The Rise and Fall of the Planning Ideal.* Chichester: Wiley & Sons.

Darley, G. (2007). *Villages of Vision: A Study of Strange Utopias.* Nottingham: Five Leaves.

Hall, P. (2014). *Cities of Tomorrow: An Intellectual History of Urban Planning and Design Since 1880,* 4th edn. Hoboken: Wiley-Blackwell.

In this chapter we unpack concepts of health and well-being and further reflect on health inequalities across different ages and groups in society. Such understanding is critical for built environment professionals endeavouring to enable people to live healthy, flourishing lives.

—

Introduction

In Chapter 1, we considered the ways in which humans have developed an understanding of links between health and the environment around them. It began with an exploration of special places that were associated with physical and spiritual healing, and ended with a consideration of ways to design the built environment to encourage healthier living.

Chapter 1 also highlighted that there are direct and indirect environmental impacts on human health and well-being. In this chapter we explore contemporary definitions of health, well-being and related terminology, and begin to unpack impacts and influences – both physical and psychological – at different life stages and for different groups in society.

—

Trends in health

A wide range of factors influence human health and well-being, from individual genetics and lifestyles through to global-level issues, such as climate change and – as highlighted by COVID-19 in 2020 – the threat of pandemics. Globally, over

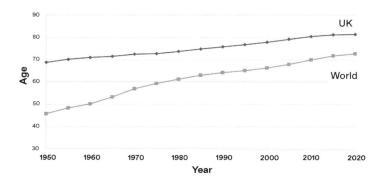

↑
Figure 2.1
Trends in average life expectancy – global and UK comparison

the last five decades, health has been improving and life expectancy has been increasing (Fig.2.1). Once-fatal diseases are now treatable and child mortality in particular has been decreasing. While positive in themselves, these trends are not without issues for societies. For example, while there is a growing proportion of older people who are active and healthy, the number susceptible to a range of physical and mental issues associated with ageing – and who might need specialist care – has also increased. Ageing societies also pose challenges in relation to sourcing adequate funding for health and social care, since the proportion of wage earners contributing to pension funds and paying taxes also decreases unless the retirement age is constantly raised.

The UK has mainly followed positive global health trends, although, as discussed below, health improvements have slowed over the most recent decade. Moreover, while physical health has generally been improving, the number of people reporting mental health problems in the UK has actually been increasing. Gains in health have also not been experienced equally across society, and while wealthier communities have benefitted greatly, in many poorer communities there is the increasing burden of those living with infirmity and chronic disease. For a sustainable future, therefore, we need to enable everyone in society – as much as possible – to live to enjoy a healthy older age. This raises the question: what exactly does it mean to be 'healthy'?

—

Defining health and well-being

Health

The most widely accepted definition of health was set out by the World Health Organization (WHO) just after the end of the Second World War. It states that health is 'a state of complete physical, mental and social well-being and not merely the absence of disease or infirmity' (WHO, 1946). Moreover, the declaration goes on to say that health is one of the fundamental rights of every person, no matter what their race, religion, political beliefs or personal background. This is an ambitious statement steeped in the optimism of the time and sets health in the broadest context – physical, mental and social. However, it should be noted that in research, even today, the term 'health' is sometimes used as a measure of *bodily condition* – that is, whether the body is suffering illness or infirmity – so readers always need to consider the way in which an author is using the term and not assume that it is the WHO definition that is being applied.

The health profession is divided between those who focus on individual human health, for example, clinicians and surgeons, and those who focus on community health. The latter are grouped under the broad heading of 'public health'; and epidemiology, the study of disease and health conditions in specified populations, is the key discipline that underpins this part of the health profession. Since urban designers and planners tend to work at the community level, in matters of health they are most likely to find themselves engaging with public health colleagues. Such interdisciplinary working can be highly rewarding, but also throws up certain challenges, and these are addressed later in the chapter.

Finally, before concluding the topic of defining health, the term 'environmental health' is also worth mentioning. Defined by WHO as those aspects of human health and disease that are determined by factors in the environment, it is largely concerned with preventing, or protecting against, anything that might cause harm where people live, work, and so on. In the UK, environmental health officers, for example, work closely with 'out of home' food supply (restaurants, takeaways, and so on) and so are ideally placed to try to increase the healthiness of these food sources – a topic discussed in Chapter 4.

Well-being and flourishing

Well-being is sometimes used as a synonym for health and sometimes as an expansive term used in conjunction with it: the phrase 'health and well-being' is commonly used to imply positive physical and mental states. It has also been suggested that well-being offers a de-medicalised concept of health (Statham and Chase, 2010). However, the term and even the spelling (well-being/wellbeing) is also disputed; so again, when engaging with texts on well-being, caution is needed.

Psychologists endeavouring to define well-being draw on two overarching concepts, or attributes – these are the hedonic and eudaimonic. Definitions of hedonic are sometimes referred to as relating to subjective well-being (Diener, 1984) and are based on people's satisfaction with life – or, put simply, their 'happiness'. In this tradition, maximising one's happiness equates to maximising one's well-being. 'Happiness' has become a major focus globally and the first *World Happiness Report* was published in April 2012, in response to a United Nations General Assembly resolution (Helliwell, Layard and Sachs, 2019). The key emphasis for this report was to depart from more traditional ways of measuring the progress of nations, for example, based on Gross Domestic Product (GDP) and economic growth. However, happiness as a measure, which is generally self-reported, is not without issues.

The eudaimonic perspective points out that people's reports of being 'happy' do not necessarily mean that they are psychologically well (Waterman, 1993). The eudaimonic conceptualisation of well-being is not so much an emotional condition as it is a process of fulfilling one's potential and living as one was inherently intended to live (Deci and Ryan, 2008), a view that can be traced back to the writings of Aristotle. Many researchers point out that in practice that there is a fair degree of overlap between hedonic and eudaimonic measures and, for example, if someone reaches their full potential, they will undoubtedly experience happiness and satisfaction with life, even if the reverse may not be necessarily true.

Taking all these aspects into consideration, we might usefully think of well-being as a kind of barometer of people's lives, a dynamic measure of an infinitely changeable interaction of personal circumstances, relationships with others *and* the physical, cultural and technological environments in which we lead our lives. This has been encapsulated into the concept of a 'languishing-to-flourishing' continuum (Keyes, 2002). The concept of human flourishing – living a rich, fulfilling life – has begun to have wider currency, with calls for urban design to embrace the concept as its overarching aim (Townshend, 2021).

Disease and illness

Before leaving our discussion on terminology, it is worth considering the terms 'disease', 'illness', 'morbidity' and 'mortality', as these often turn up in health and well-being studies and are referred to in later sections of this book. Firstly, a 'disease' refers to a disordered or incorrectly functioning organ, structure or system of the body. Diseases have symptoms that enable them to be identified by the medical profession. Illness is sometimes used as a synonym for 'disease' but can also refer to a more personal perception of one's health, and people may refer to 'feeling ill' when they have no identifiable disease. Morbidity refers to the condition of suffering from a disease and also the rate of disease within a population; for example, as discussed in Chapter 3, higher levels of air pollution are associated with increased morbidity from respiratory diseases. Lastly, mortality refers to the rate of death; for example, again as discussed in Chapter 3, road traffic accidents are the highest cause of mortality among 15–29-year-olds in the UK.

Lifestyle diseases
Finally, the term 'lifestyle disease' has become increasingly common in health research. Lifestyle diseases are a category of conditions and diseases that are attributable, at least in part, to the lifestyle led by the individual. For example, obesity, although a condition with a complex aetiology,[1] frequently results from eating a poor diet and taking too little exercise; though what *causes* a person to follow these patterns of behaviour is debated. Obesity, in turn, is a condition which has been linked to a range of lifestyle health problems and diseases, including type-2 diabetes, hypertension, heart disease, stroke and some cancers.

—

Health, well-being and the life-course
The influence of the environment at different life stages is an important issue. Age changes our physical and mental relationship with space, sometimes in ways the individual has little control over. Adverse environmental conditions may be particularly impactful at different life stages. Also, for example, since some age groups, such as older adults and the very young, tend to be less mobile, environmental qualities found in the home neighbourhood environment may be more important for these groups than others. By contrast, with very mobile groups, the sum of environmental influences – those from home, work and leisure amenities, and travel in between these locations – requires consideration.

Childhood
Arguably, environmental impacts begin before birth as, for example, exposure to pollution, or living under stressful conditions, may harm a developing baby. A nutritious diet, with consumption of fresh fruit and vegetables, is essential during

pregnancy for a healthy baby's development. However, where fresh produce is difficult to obtain, or where people are living in a neighbourhood saturated with fast food outlets, an appropriate diet may be much harder to achieve.

Young children are particularly prone to environmental influences because their bodies are developing rapidly. In Chapter 5, we highlight that exposure to a range of 'natural'[2] environments at a young age is important in developing a healthy immune system. More generally, adequate, safe, outside space for exercise and developing socialisation during play is also vital for healthy childhood development. In Chapter 3 we address how traffic can be particularly detrimental to children. Where parents fear danger from traffic it means they are much less likely to allow children to walk or cycle to school, or even to play outside.

Children who live physically constrained lives may develop more slowly, have strained relationships with their parents and have poorer social skills than children who are able to play freely outside. Moreover, children who are not physically active are more likely to become overweight, even obese – with serious health consequences that may track through to adulthood.

However, being outside may also carry risk; exposure to air pollution is a key factor in childhood asthma which has dramatically increased in most developed nations, including the UK. Some research has linked exposure to high levels of air pollution in early life with delinquent behaviour in adolescence and even serious long-term mental health problems in later life (Haynes et al., 2011). Excessive noise disturbance – for example, from traffic – is also a cause for concern and may affect a child's ability to concentrate at school. Sleep is important for development in childhood, and neighbourhood noise causing lack of sleep is in turn associated with behavioural issues such as hyperactivity (Tiesler et al., 2013). Childhood issues can also track through to later life, even if they are subsequently addressed; and this means that environmental influences on children's lives are particularly important. Finally, children in poorer neighbourhoods have a much greater risk of being impacted by issues such as poor air quality, so that health inequalities – the unfair and avoidable differences in health between different sections of the population – are set in train at a young age.

Adolescence

Adolescence is the period between puberty and adulthood (approximately 13–18 years of age) and is also an important life stage to consider in relation to environmental influence, as it usually represents a period of increasing freedom and self-determination. Adolescents also have a great deal of 'free' time to fill up – this can be up to 50 per cent of their waking hours – and only so much can be occupied by constructive pastimes (Larson, 2000). This means they tend to spend a great deal of time simply 'hanging out' in public spaces, such as parks, or even on the streets. However, their presence is quite often not welcomed in these settings and interventions are used to effectively 'design out' this age group – for example, anti-skateboarding measures – with the result that their needs are often overlooked. This may lead them to venture into inappropriate and even hazardous places such as abandoned structures, which carry a risk of physical injury.

By this stage, neurological systems are fully developed and are less vulnerable to exposure to hazards such as pollution, by comparison with younger age groups. However, psychological influences from the character of the neighbourhood may be heightened. Some researchers highlight influences on deviant behaviour in this age group in neighbourhoods where there is an underlying presence of social disorder that also manifests itself in the built environment. The so-called 'broken windows theory' suggests that small acts of vandalism and incivilities such as litter and graffiti may encourage more serious criminal acts (Keizer, Lindenberg and Steg, 2008). Alternatively, neighbourhoods with high levels of social cohesion – meaning the connectedness and solidarity of neighbourhood residents, a topic we explore in Chapter 5 – demonstrate lower levels of deviant behaviour in this age group (Gilbert and Galea, 2014).

Adulthood

Some environmental impacts track through different life stages. Air pollution, for example, is also associated with adult asthma, heart disease and increased risk of cancer. Noise pollution is associated with negative impacts on mental performance, stress and anxiety, and studies have also associated noise disturbance with high blood pressure and heart disease (Münzel et al., 2014). Similarly, some influences that begin in adolescence continue into adulthood. Living in neighbourhoods that exhibit high levels of incivility such as litter, graffiti and vandalism has been linked to issues such as depression and substance abuse in adulthood (Burdette, Hill and Hale, 2011). A poor neighbourhood environment is also one of a series of factors linked to increased sedentary behaviour – along with car-domination, lack of green space, and so on; these are explored in detail in Chapter 3. The availability and accessibility of outlets that enable harmful behaviours – such as payday loan and betting shops, cut-price alcohol and tobacco outlets, and nutritionally poor fast food – also increase risk of indebtedness, stress, poor mental health, substance addiction and obesity (Townshend, 2017).

As with adolescence, greater social cohesion within the neighbourhood setting is associated with reduced risk of mental health problems. Furthermore, as explored in Chapter 5, greener neighbourhoods are associated with reduced mental health problems in adults, as well as encouraging greater levels of physical activity. However, a further issue that we explore in Chapter 3 is that many adults live mobile and complex lives, meaning that the home neighbourhood may be less influential than one that surrounds the workplace, or where leisure time is spent. In considering environmental impacts and influence in adulthood, it is important, therefore, to consider these multiple environments and serial or cumulative exposures.

Older age

As stated at the beginning of this section, in older age, life-worlds often begin to shrink and older people become increasingly dependent on the neighbourhood surrounding their home. When opportunities are restricted, places to go out to see and meet neighbours – for example, a local park – can be particularly important in combating isolation and loneliness, as well as ensuring older adults get essential physical exercise. Interaction with others is vital to maintaining positive mental functioning. In neighbourhoods with a strong sense of social cohesion, older people are more likely, therefore, to report positive well-being (Stafford, McMunn and De Vogli, 2011). Alternatively, low levels of social interaction can contribute to depression, poor mental health, the onset of dementia and other neurological disorders (Read, Comas-Herrera and Grundy, 2020).

Feeling safe in one's neighbourhood has a heightened impact in the older age group, even though older people are generally at a relatively low risk of crime. If an older person feels vulnerable, they may effectively shut themselves off inside their home, again causing feelings of isolation and leading to poor mental health. In this age group, the presence of litter and evidence of vandalism can particularly influence perceptions of safety. Poor maintenance of pavements and general clutter and litter in the street can also increase the risk – real and perceived – of trips and falls, further discouraging older people from spending time outside. Finally, the physical impacts of air quality and noise disturbance at this stage in life also seem to be implicated in the onset of cognitive impairment, memory loss and dementia (Clark, Crumpler and Notley, 2020).

—
Health inequalities and deprivation

It has long been established that health and well-being have a sharply defined socio-economic profile. While particular environmental influences change over the life course, socio-economic status (SES) remains a constant factor in a person's health and well-being. The health of babies born into poorer communities is more likely to be adversely impacted by environmental factors, and that holds true at all life stages, including older age. Moreover, the socio-economic dynamic operates at all spatial scales – globally, nationally and even within cities themselves. In the UK, people in poor neighbourhoods die, on average, seven years earlier than those living in wealthy ones and are more likely to spend a larger part of their shortened lives coping with a debilitating illness, or a physical or mental disability (Marmot et al., 2010; Ellaway et al., 2012). In some cities the average life expectancy between poor and rich neighbourhoods can differ by over 10 years. Direct economic influences – for example, being able to afford a better diet, access to private healthcare, and so on – explain much of the differential; however, not all of it can be explained away in this manner.

As outlined in the key life stages section above, environmental quality is a major risk factor in poorer neighbourhoods, with poorer areas more likely to suffer from higher ambient air pollution (often linked to traffic levels, as outlined in Chapter 3), higher levels of graffiti, fly-tipped waste and litter, and generally poorer levels of cleanliness and maintenance. Housing quality is also a key issue and this is specifically addressed in Chapter 4.

Of great concern in the UK, health inequalities seem to be increasing, rather than decreasing, with recent national reviews (known – by the name of their author – as Marmot reviews) in 2010 and 2020 showing worrying trends (see Marmot et al., 2010; Marmot et al., 2020). For example, while life expectancy increased in the decade to 2020, it was only at half the rate of the previous decade, showing a slowdown that is particularly acute in poorer communities (Marmot et al., 2020). London, as the wealthiest region in England, showed the greatest increases in life expectancy. Moreover, while in every region life expectancy increased for the most advantaged area decile (the top 10 per cent), by contrast, life expectancy for women in the most deprived decile actually *decreased* in most regions, except for in London, the West Midlands and the north-west. Men in the most deprived decile did not fare much better, with life expectancy decreases occurring in several regions.

A related issue to total life expectancy is that of disability-free life expectancy, sometimes referred to as healthy life expectancy (HLE) – that is, the number of years people live

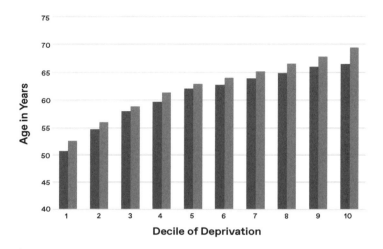

Inequalities in disability-free life expectancy in England – decile 1 being
the most deprived communities and decile 10 the least deprived

Note: dark grey = women; lighter grey = men.

without a debilitating and life-constraining condition. Though the
socio-economic profiles of total life expectancy and healthy life
expectancy follow the same pattern, the socio-economic profiling
of healthy life expectancy is more pronounced, meaning that
people in poorer communities not only live shorter lives, but can
expect to live less of that shorter life free of a significant health
problem (a 'life-limiting condition', in the terms of the report).
As Figure 2.2 shows, a man in one of the least deprived areas of
England can expect to live an astonishing 18.7 years longer without
a life-limiting condition than a woman in the most deprived areas.

Marmot concludes that socio-economic factors lie behind
these circumstances, with the poorest areas having the highest
preventable mortality rates, while the wealthiest have the lowest;
however, as already outlined, socio-economic factors and
environmental quality are deeply intertwined. It is therefore in
poorer areas where environmental interventions have the greatest
potential for positive impact.

From inequalities to the Settlement Health Map

In 1991, Dahlgren and Whitehead published their (subsequently much-cited) paper exploring solutions to health inequalities – which, as highlighted above, have further diverged since their work. The authors describe a social-ecological theory of health and map out the layered relationship between individuals, their environment and their health influences (Fig.2.3). At the heart of the model, the genetic make-up, age, gender and ethnicity of the individual determines many aspects of their health. Surrounding this, lifestyle factors such as diet, physical activity level, smoking, alcohol consumption, and so on, will also impact health. The next layer, social and community influences, focuses on whether individuals have friends and family who can offer support mechanisms in times of difficulty. Beyond this are the individual's living and working conditions, and finally, the general socio-economic conditions of the place where they live.

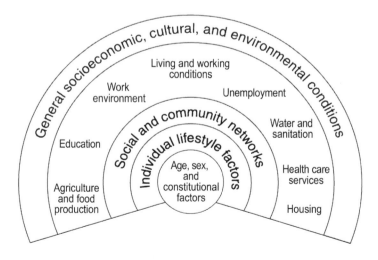

↑
Figure 2.3
Social determinants of health

In focus: Settlement Health Map

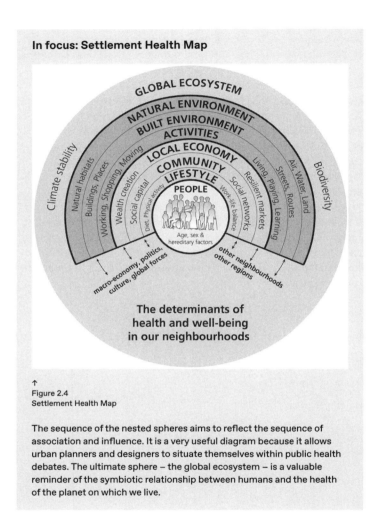

The determinants of
health and well-being
in our neighbourhoods

↑
Figure 2.4
Settlement Health Map

The sequence of the nested spheres aims to reflect the sequence of
association and influence. It is a very useful diagram because it allows
urban planners and designers to situate themselves within public health
debates. The ultimate sphere – the global ecosystem – is a valuable
reminder of the symbiotic relationship between humans and the health
of the planet on which we live.

These relationships were later reconfigured and developed
by Barton and Grant in their Settlement Health Map (Fig.2.4),
which shows health influences as a set of nested spheres (2006;
Barton, Grant and Guise, 2010). The map was taken up at a

global level by the WHO Healthy Cities Movement and is now widely adopted in public health and urban planning documents. Again, individuals are at the heart of the map, surrounded by their lifestyle and the nature of the community in which they live, including its economic activity. The map specifically highlights the influence of the built environment, which goes beyond buildings and other structures to include all man-made elements found in cities, such as parks and other open spaces. It is within this sphere that urban planners and designers have their most direct impact – though arguably they might also work in, or influence, other spheres such as community, local economy and even the natural environment.

Like all good models, the Settlement Health Map manages to capture complex relationships in an accessible way. Moreover, as outlined by the authors, the map can be used in various ways, not least as an analytical framework to interrogate urban design and planning decision-making. For example, for any policy or project, the impact on each of the inner spheres – People, Lifestyles, Community, Economy, Activities – and outer spheres – Natural Environments and Global Ecosystems – should be analysed. Put another way, this allows consideration of everything, from whether a policy or project improves individual lives, to whether it protects or potentially harms the planet, and the interplay of, and with, every stage in between. It therefore provides a useful departure point for any project, real or imagined.

—
WHO Healthy Cities Network

As stated above, the Settlement Health Map has become a widely adopted symbol of the World Health Organization (WHO) Healthy Cities Network. This was launched in 1986 as part of the WHO 'healthy settings' approach, which in turn has its roots in the Ottawa Charter for Health Promotion (WHO, 1986). The central aim of the programme is to raise awareness of public health and to promote the need for interdisciplinary action. According to Hancock and Duhl – who were key to launching the healthy cities programme – the concepts are broad and incorporate ideas from sociology, human geography, urban planning, ecology, philosophy and other disciplines, in addition to public health (Hancock and Duhl, 1988).

In summary, the WHO Healthy Cities project calls on planners, designers, public health professionals and others to work together to address health concerns. In Europe, the Healthy Cities Network has grown rapidly, with around 1,400 municipalities currently involved in 30 different countries, including seven designated cities in the UK. Copenhagen, a founding member of the Healthy Cities Network, is well known as an exemplar of health-focused planning and design, with exceptional facilities for cycling and many other forms of physical activity 'designed in' to the city – for example, Copenhill power station which incorporates a ski-slope and various other sports and recreation facilities, including the world's highest climbing wall (Visit Copenhagen, 2021). However, in the UK such dramatic interventions have yet to materialise, and the larger city members of the network – Liverpool, Newcastle and Belfast – have yet to significantly deliver on their healthy city status. Moreover, Liverpool and Newcastle are major cities within regions with particularly poor health profiles.

—

The challenges of interdisciplinary working
By now it should have become clear that urban designers and planners need to work closely with public health bodies and a host of other professions in order to reduce the negative impacts of the built environment on health and well-being, and to reduce, rather than exacerbate, health inequalities. The WHO Healthy Cities programme is a good example of where that is happening, and as will become apparent in later chapters, there are a number of initiatives working at various spatial scales to drive this interdisciplinary agenda forward. However, there are still significant challenges in reaching full potential in this regard.

Traditionally, academic disciplines have thrived by developing claims over particular areas of knowledge, each accompanied by its own culture, ethos and even language (McNeely and

Wolverton, 2008). The sciences, arts and humanities – in many ways themselves artificial divisions of knowledge – are sub-divided into subjects such as physics, architecture and sociology, and each of these have been sub-divided again and again into various specialisms. Universities have traditionally followed this logic in terms of their organisational, and even funding, regimes.

These structures continue to frame professional education. For example, despite the common foundations identified in Chapter 1, in a modern university, those trained in public health and urban planning will be taught in completely different faculties and rarely, if ever, find themselves in the same lecture theatre. Vocational courses can be particularly constricted by the pragmatics of professional accreditation. This has a knock-on effect in professional practice and in public institutions, where it generates what is often referred to as 'silo' thinking.

The issue of evidence
A key issue in relation to interdisciplinary working in the health and built environment professions is what is understood as evidence, meaning the empirical underpinnings of any action or intervention. Public health practitioners are used to medical science approaches, such as randomised control trials (RCTs). An RCT is an experiment that aims to reduce sources of bias when testing the effectiveness of new interventions, such as a new medication. For example, human volunteers testing a new drug might be randomly allocated into two groups. One group is subjected to the medication that is being assessed, while the other group receives a placebo. The whole exercise is conducted under carefully prescribed conditions to avoid confounding factors; results are generated by comparing the groups' measured response. Trials will then be repeated for validation purposes.

Clearly, in terms of medical treatments this approach makes perfect sense. However, this type of evidence is almost impossible to generate in relation to the built environment. Interventions in the built environment are generally permanent –

or at least difficult to change/reverse – and cannot be controlled under laboratory conditions. Urban planners and designers therefore rely on other types of evidence – for example, the interpretation of relatively small numbers provided by in-depth, qualitative interviews. This kind of evidence can seem quite alien to public health practitioners. Designers and planners also utilise precedent studies – the examination of what has worked elsewhere. These should always include detailed examination of the transferability of such evidence; however, this is not always the case.

Problems around evidence, as well as culture and language, in studies of the built environment are not insurmountable, but require patience and understanding. They also require extra time and resources to be built into projects in order to allow mutual understanding to develop between the professions. However, given that, particularly in the public sector, resources are often already squeezed, this is a challenge in its own right.

——

Conclusions

While there is a widely accepted, established definition of health, well-being has a more disputed meaning. However, caution is required in engaging with texts on both health and well-being from different disciplines, as terminology may be used inconsistently. Substantially, the following issues are of concern to urban design and planning:

1 *Age*   Environmental impacts on health and well-being may vary over the life course. However, adverse impacts can track through from childhood into adulthood, even when they have been addressed.
2 *Mobility*   Less mobile groups, such as older adults and the very young, experience greater impacts from the environmental conditions in their home neighbourhood than more mobile groups. Conversely, the sum of environmental influences in the multiple environments in which mobile adults live out their lives require consideration.

3 *Socio-economic profile*   Health and well-being have sharply defined socio-economic profiles. People from poorer communities in the UK not only have shorter lives but are more likely to suffer from a debilitating disease or condition for a longer proportion of their lives than wealthier people. Concerningly, health inequalities between rich and poor in the UK seem to be on the increase.

There is now more interdisciplinary working between the health and built environment professions than has been the case for many decades. However, much more is needed to address contemporary health and well-being issues.

Further reading

Barton, H. and M. Grant (2006). 'A Health Map for the Local Human Habitat', *Journal of the Royal Society for the Promotion of Health* 126(6), pp 252–3.

Corburn, J. (2015). 'Urban Inequities, Population Health and Spatial Planning'. In: H. Barton, S. Thompson, S. Burgess and M. Grant (eds), *The Routledge Handbook of Planning for Health and Well-being*. London: Routledge.

Gilbert, E. and S. Galea (2014). 'Urban Neighborhoods and Mental Health Across the Life Course'. In: R. Cooper et al., *Wellbeing: A Complete Reference Guide Volume II – Wellbeing and the Environment*. Chichester: Wiley Blackwell.

Marmot, M., J. Allen, T. Boyce, P. Goldblatt and J. Morrison (2020). *Health Equity in England: The Marmot Review 10 Years On*. London: Institute of Health Equity.

In this chapter we overview the health impacts of our sedentary, car-dominated cities and ponder whether we can return to more active modes of transport, and if so, how?

Introduction

People need access to education, work, cultural and leisure activities if they are going to live healthy, fulfilling lives. However, in contemporary cities facilities are often spread apart. This means people spend considerable time and resources travelling from one place to another. The problem is that this travel has increasingly become a car-borne activity, and this is harmful to human and planetary health.

Electronic access is a huge boon to contemporary living, and many people have vast virtual resources available from home. However, people also have a limited capacity for how much time they can spend indoors (highlighted by the COVID-19 crisis) and so some travel will always be desirable. Enabling as much of this movement as possible to be 'active', and therefore healthy, is a significant challenge.

The journey to car domination

Before the 20th century, cities were designed around the needs of the pedestrian. Owning a horse-drawn carriage was only an option for the wealthy, and this situation changed little in the early days of motorised transport. Early private cars were expensive and required an experienced mechanic to maintain them. Mass car ownership famously began in the USA with the Ford Model T (1908 onwards); however, in the UK, even by the beginning of the 1950s, 80 per cent of households had no car.

The early post-Second World War period was, however, one of rapid change. The economy boomed and demand for consumer goods, including cars, increased. Moreover, city planning was transformed. As outlined in Chapter 1, modernist planning principles sought to separate cities out into different zones of work, home, recreation and transport. Cities began to be much more spread out. Commercial and public services also saw opportunities to exploit car-borne transportation and achieve economies of scale by investing in fewer city centres. 'Out-of-town', with plenty of parking, became the new location of choice.

Subsequently, and as cost reduced, car ownership boomed, and in a reversal from the 1950s, now 80 per cent of UK households have a car and many have more than one. For many

↑
Figure 3.1
Many urban roads are constantly choked with traffic

people, cars have become an essential 'must-have', an extension of their personality and a statement about their lifestyle and aspirations. Additionally, as society has embraced the car, other modes of transportation have largely been ignored, investment withdrawn and their decline viewed as inevitable.

Yet cars have not brought about the freedom our forebears dreamed of. Cars are space-hungry, requiring vast amounts of infrastructure to accommodate them. They are also a self-perpetuating commodity. The more you provide for them, the more people use them. However, there is only so much land available and both inter- and intra-urban roads in the UK are often choked with traffic (Fig.3.1). We may think cars have provided us with freedom, mobility and access to opportunities, but in many ways, they are a disaster for human and planetary health.

—

The health impacts of motor vehicles

The negative health impacts of motor vehicles – and particularly private cars – are surprisingly varied. Pollution regularly hits media headlines and vehicular pollution is a killer; however, some issues are more insidious, as examined below.

Sedentary lifestyles

Sedentary lifestyles are a global issue and a huge concern since they are a key factor in burgeoning rates of obesity and many non-communicable diseases (NCDs). WHO now rates physical inactivity as the fourth leading cause of global mortality (WHO, 2009). The links between habitual vehicle use, weight gain and associated health risks have been established for some time; however, as with many aspects of environment and behaviour, the causal pathways are complex.

Driving contributes to sedentary lifestyles in many ways. As a mode of transport it effectively locks us into a sedentary, seated position for the entire journey. This is not so in alternative forms of transportation, which require some form of physical activity, even if that is walking to a nearby bus stop. Sedentary behaviours are reinforcing and, particularly for those who drive long distances, there is a correlation with unhealthy lifestyle choices. These include screen time (TV or computer use), smoking, poor diet and insufficient sleep. Only one healthier lifestyle factor is related to regular driving – lower reported alcohol consumption, undoubtedly due to strict drink-driving laws (Mackay et al., 2019).

However, car use is not just a sedentary activity; it consumes resources (time, land and money) that could be available for physical activity. In the UK, around half of all adults fail to meet physical activity guidelines, and having too little time is an important factor. Also, because car transport requires large amounts of land and infrastructure, this diverts investment away from healthier alternatives. Provision for cars further hinders more active travel (walking and cycling) by making these activities unpleasant and unsafe for those who might otherwise choose to undertake them.

Air pollution
Rated by WHO as the polluter of most concerning source (Henschel, Chan and WHO, 2013), there is a large body of evidence on the health effects of 'traffic-related air pollution' (TRAP). In the UK, motorised transport currently accounts for around a third of all emissions of carbon dioxide, the 'greenhouse' gas that is driving climate change, which is a huge health concern. TRAP includes carbon monoxide, hydrocarbons, nitrogen oxides (NO_x) (which causes lung irritation and weakens the body's defences against respiratory infections), particulate matter (PM) (ultrafine particles less than a tenth of a human hair in width), and various other toxins. Most PM is discharged in exhaust gas; however, PM also includes resuspended road dust, tyre and brake particles.

The various TRAP pollutants have been associated with different types of health problems, and causal pathways are, again, complex. Living near a busy road, for example, has been associated with the onset of asthma, or worsening of the condition in children who are already asthmatic. More generally, studies have suggested links to problems with lung function in all ages related to nitrogen oxides (Matz et al., 2019).

PM has been specifically linked to heart disease, through a process known as atherosclerosis, or clogging of the arteries. PM is so fine that it can enter the blood stream when inhaled, and it also deposits itself deep within the lungs. High traffic situations such as traffic jams, or queues waiting at traffic lights, are known to increase PM concentrations, and while people spend a limited time commuting, these periods show spikes in individuals' absorption. There is also evidence that car drivers are more at risk from traffic pollution than pedestrians and cyclists in the same environment because exhaust gases are sucked in through car ventilation systems. Finally, TRAP has been associated with allergies, certain cancers and dementia in older age.

Noise pollution
Noise pollution from traffic goes hand in hand with air pollution. As such, it is somewhat difficult to disentangle the evidence around the two issues. Chronic noise exposure is, however, correlated with specific health problems including sleep disturbance, cognitive impairment among children, annoyance, stress-related mental health risks, tinnitus and heart disease. There is further evidence that associates road noise with increased risk of dementia in older age and finds that traffic noise adversely impacts the poorest in society, adding to health inequalities (Science for Environment Policy, 2016).

Flooding and water pollution
Flooding and water pollution are somewhat overlooked in relation to road transport. However, the greater the expanse of hard surface, the less open ground available to absorb rainfall. Even at the domestic scale, in suburban areas, what were front gardens have often been given over to car parking, causing run-off (excess surface water), which was once largely unheard of. Run-off in turn can overload water treatment services. In the US, research has found spikes in outbreaks of E-coli infection after floods. More generally, however, flooding of residential areas is a traumatic experience for individuals and communities, and the psychological impacts can last many decades.

Death and injury

Latest UK figures (for 2018) show that over 26,600 people were killed or seriously injured on the roads over a 12-month period, with 1,770 fatalities (Department for Transport, 2018). Deaths from road accidents have reduced significantly from a peak in the mid-1960s. However, much of this is to do with increasingly safer technology within the car to protect the driver and passengers, and externally, car construction is less deadly to pedestrians and cyclists. Injuries from road traffic accidents are still the leading cause of death among people aged between 15 and 29 years of age in the UK.

Increased stress levels

The links between driving and stress have been known about since the 1950s, and research continues to show that drivers who spend more than two hours on the road each day are more likely to report higher psychological distress and lower quality of life. Moreover, these factors are again associated with other poor health behaviours such as smoking and physical inactivity, and outcomes such as obesity and poor mental health (Ding et al., 2014).

Community severance

Community severance refers to divisive effects that busy roads have on those communities that live either side of them. While there are no studies reporting a direct link to health outcomes, the impact is likely to exacerbate issues such as social isolation and loneliness, as those impacted may be put off from accessing facilities and social networks which would otherwise be within easy reach (Duncan, 2011). In turn, these issues can have serious long-term effects on mental health.

—

Health inequalities and traffic

Not only is road transport unhealthy, but it is also a major contributor to health inequalities (see Chapter 2). Car dominance can restrict access to opportunities for those who cannot afford a car, impeding their access to employment. Moreover, some of the most congested roads run through poorer inner urban areas, causing the worst effects of air pollution and noise to be inflicted on them. Finally, such adverse impacts from congestion and pollution can prevent poorer communities from walking and cycling because such activities are too unpleasant or dangerous. Death and injury from traffic impacts the poorest in society to a disproportionate degree. For example, in the UK, children in the 10 per cent of most deprived wards are four times more likely to be hit by a car than those in the least deprived (Grayling et al., 2002). This cumulation of multiple problems and disadvantage in poorer communities is sometimes referred to as 'deprivation amplification'.

—

Technological 'fixes' for transport health challenges

Road transport is, of course, undergoing fundamental changes in terms of energy sources and traffic management in our urban centres. Before moving on to consider more active modes of transportation, it is worth considering how these may impact health and well-being in the future.

Switching to electric vehicles

The UK government plans to ban the sale of petrol and diesel vehicles by 2035. This should have positive impacts on air and noise pollution since electric vehicles do not emit exhaust fumes and are much quieter. However, millions of petrol and diesel vehicles will still be on the roads. There are no plans to scrap these vehicles and there is no reliable modelling available for how long it will take for all vehicles with combustion engines to be replaced, meaning that associated pollution will continue long into the future.

Concerns have also been raised about electric vehicles themselves. For example, while they do not emit exhaust gas, they still produce other types of PM from braking, road dust, and so on. Moreover, whether enough renewable energy is available to meet demand from vehicles is debatable, especially

↑
Figure 3.2
Electric vehicles are still space/infrastructure hungry – here, three parking
bays have been turned into two charging points

at peak times – for example, after work in the evening, when
many people will want to charge their cars.

As stated, electric vehicles are considerably quieter,
potentially addressing noise pollution. However, at low speeds
(20kmph) they are so quiet that there is considerable debate
about whether some noise is desirable from a safety perspective,
so that pedestrians can hear vehicles coming. This may mean
noise reduction will be less pronounced than it might otherwise
have been. More fundamentally, however, they still require the
same large amount of road space/infrastructure (Fig.3.2) – and
the same minimal energy expenditure from humans.

Robust data concerning the impact on health from switching
to electric vehicles is currently unavailable. However, considering
the overall impacts of current modes of transport on health and
well-being, it would seem likely that the planned introduction of
electric vehicles will bring modest improvements at best for the
foreseeable future.

Low Emission Zones and Clean Air Zones

London has had a Low Emission Zone (LEZ) since 2008 (this is now London-wide) and an Ultra-Low Emission Zone (ULEZ) from 2019 in the central area (again due for expansion in 2021). Essentially, these are geographically defined areas where vehicles must meet certain emissions standards, and owners face charges or fines if they operate non-compliant vehicles. While outside of London the term 'Clean Air Zone' (CAZ) is being used, the principle is the same, although details vary. CAZs or LEZs will be required in all major urban areas by 2022 (Gov.UK, 2019).

In principle LEZs/CAZs are an important contribution to reducing air pollution and encouraging cleaner transport and 'active travel' (examined in the following section). But here again, there is a lack of robust evidence of impact. Most CAZs are too new, or yet to be initiated. Early research on London's LEZ, however, is somewhat disappointing. Vehicle operators have certainly reduced the number of older, more polluting vehicles, and freight services have switched from larger lorries to lighter vans. However, PM reductions have remained modest and NO_x reductions hardly discernible (Ellis, Greaves and Hensher, 2013). While stricter controls and larger areas covered by regulation should improve this picture, the evidence (as with electric vehicles) suggests that for a healthier future, the key is to dramatically reduce vehicle miles travelled.

Car-sharing schemes

As with traffic management schemes above, car-sharing schemes – informal, self-organised and commercial – have the potential for health benefits if they reduce the number of cars on the road and the number of miles travelled by individuals in cars. Evidence is limited; however, it might be expected that members of car-sharing schemes would make fewer journeys by car than owner/drivers. This is because, however 'easy access' schemes are, journeys need to be booked in advance, which may reduce impulse trips. Furthermore, upfront per-trip costs are apparent, meaning people may be more judicious in their car use, and active travel (walking and cycling) alternatives may seem more attractive (Duncan, 2011).

Car-sharing also introduces an active travel element (however small) because there will be a trip on foot to wherever the car is stored. Again, evidence is limited; however, analysis of travel patterns in London revealed that people in households that do not own a car were more than three times as likely to undertake 30 minutes of active travel per day than their car-owning equivalents (Ellis, Greaves and Hensher, 2013).

Car-sharing schemes may, therefore, provide an important contribution to healthier lifestyle choices and help develop a more sophisticated use for car transport, so that it is only used when strictly necessary. This would be, for example, when heavy items are also being transported, when distances are too far to walk or cycle and/or are not well served by public transport alternatives. However, currently, any benefits are still more potential than realised.

—

Active travel

Schemes to reduce car dependence are part of the solution in terms of promoting healthier, more active lives; however, the other is the effective promotion of walking and cycling in cities – this is referred to as 'active travel'.

Walking

Despite our dependence on motor vehicles, walking is still the most common way for people to get about within their immediate locality, and consequently, walking is the most common type of exercise for humans; it is the basic form of active travel. It is a natural form of aerobic activity which confers multifarious benefits with minimal adverse effects and can significantly contribute to adults' recommended 150 minutes of moderate physical activity per week. Regular walking can reduce the risk of morbidity from all causes, particularly heart and lung disease, type-2 diabetes and some cancers. Walking is also good for social health. It promotes social interaction between neighbours and is socially inclusive, requiring little expenditure.

It is also important to consider that people walk both as a form of transport (utility) and as a leisure-time activity, though these intentions are sometimes carried out simultaneously. The built environment can support, or constrain, both types of walking. For example, if shops and services are within walking distance, this may influence walking for transport; if there are pleasant views, green spaces, and so on, this may support walking for pleasure.

Cycling

Cycling is the main alternative form of active travel. Arguably, modes such as skateboarding, roller skating, scootering, and so on, are also active, but the numbers involved in the UK are very small. Cycling is an even more healthy activity than walking, mainly due to the extra effort involved in cycling inclines,

↑
Figure 3.3
Cycling is safest when it has its own bespoke infrastructure provision, separate from vehicles and pedestrians

or even just pushing off from a standing start. Like walking, people cycle for utilitarian purposes as well as for pleasure, and those who cycle to work find it less stressful than their motorist counterparts. Cycling is also linked to other healthy, low-emission behaviours, for example, consuming a diet high in fruit and vegetables (Howard, 2009).

Cycling and walking are often lumped together in active travel studies, but their requirements are quite different, and one of the challenges of increasing both modes is to avoid conflict between them, especially when they have to share the same limited space. Conflict between cyclists and motor vehicles is also obviously a problem, with between 15 and 20 cyclists killed every year in London alone. Therefore, cycling is safest when is has its own – bespoke – infrastructure provision (Fig.3.3).

Active and sociable neighbourhoods

Research has suggested that areas of cities that have high residential density, contain local shops and services, have good-quality public transportation links, and where pedestrian spaces are well-maintained and highly connected, encourage active travel for both utility and leisure. These locations are often referred to with the moniker 'walkable neighbourhoods', which is a useful shorthand to distinguish areas that are not designed around the needs of the car. However, in focusing on health, a more encompassing and useful categorisation might be 'active and sociable' neighbourhoods. Neighbourhoods that were developed prior to mass car ownership and designed around the needs of the pedestrian are often naturally supportive of active travel and sociability (Fig.3.4).

However, it would be wrong to assume that all 1900s neighbourhoods are active and sociable. Some of our poorest inner-city areas have housing stock from this period. As outlined in Chapter 2, all aspects of health have a steep socio-economic gradient. The benefits of supportive city forms can easily be overridden by poverty, a subject we return to in Chapter 4. In the next sections, however, we unpack those physical elements that may support activity and sociability in more detail.

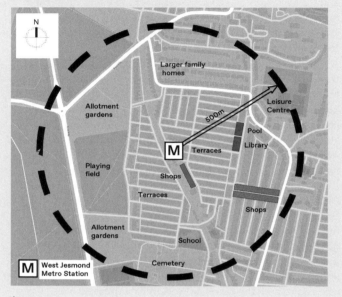

In focus: an active and sociable neighbourhood – West Jesmond, Newcastle

↑
Figure 3.4
Plan of West Jesmond, Newcastle

The plans above show the 1900s plan of West Jesmond, Newcastle. Originally served by the railway, now part of the Tyne and Wear Metro system, the area contains dense terraces nearest to the station, larger houses on the periphery and most essential shops and services within a 500-metre radius. Moreover, while the smaller houses have no gardens, occupants can rent garden allotments nearby to grow healthy fruit and vegetables. West Jesmond remains a popular residential community, appealing to both families and students.

Urban form and active travel

Key influences that have been identified as supporting active travel are *density* of population, *diversity* of destinations and pedestrian-friendly *design* – sometimes referred to as the '3 Ds' (Cerevero and Kochelman, 1997), though in reality, a fourth 'D', *distance*, is extremely important. Other authors have reframed these categories and sub-divided the themes into mixed land uses, street connectivity, residential density, transportation facilities and pedestrian infrastructure (Sallis, Millstein and Carlson, 2011); however, the thrust of argument remains unchanged. An important issue for UK research and practice, however, is that many of these studies have been conducted in North America and their transferability to the UK context requires *careful consideration*.

Residential density

Residential density is usually measured by total land area minus space taken up for roads, open space and non-residential land-use; it is often used as a proxy for population density. Density is important because local shops and services require sufficient numbers of persons within accessible distance to make them viable. In dense areas people are also more likely to see others walking and this sets up a positive cycle. The more people see others walk, the more they will consider it normal; and the safer they feel (through natural surveillance of and from others), the more likely it is that they will do it themselves.

There are also pragmatic issues. For example, in densely built-up areas, there is often a lack of parking and what exists may incur a charge; these factors add to the expense of owning a car, as well as making it less convenient. However, it must also be recognised that such high-density living may benefit some groups in society more than others. For example, students and young workers may enjoy high-density apartment living when there are facilities nearby which serve their lifestyle. However, such a situation would be a poor environment for a young family, particularly if there is a lack of suitable play space for children.

Studies have sought to correlate residential density, active travel and the ensuing health consequences. These studies suggest that very low densities – for example, less than 10 units per hectare – may be correlated to sedentary lifestyles, risk of being overweight and obesity. However, this is a very low density indeed, of a type that does not exist in urban areas in the UK. In UK outer suburban areas, for example, it is typical to find around 30 units per hectare. However, this is below the level at which local shops and services are necessarily viable – that is, around 50 units per hectare. Therefore, while density alone may not be low enough to discourage walking in many suburbs, the lack of local facilities might well be.

Diversity of land-use
Diversity of land-use is important, therefore, as it potentially provides multiple destinations to walk and cycle to. Evidence suggests correlation between non-residential land-use mix and walking. However, broader issues of 'accessibility' – these include, affordability and psychological access (whether people perceive a service is aimed at them) – will also come into play (Saelens and Handy, 2008). Land given over to public transportation as part of the local offer can even increase walking, as the first part of such a journey is naturally on foot. However, a frequent cause of frustration for cyclists is that bus and light rail services often do not allow the carriage of, or sufficient parking for, cycles.

One element of land-use diversity which is key to health and well-being is the provision of greenspace within neighbourhoods. This is of such importance that it warrants its own chapter and is, therefore, dealt with separately in Chapter 5. However, importantly, not all diversity in land-use is healthy. Clusters of unhealthy uses – such as nutritionally poor fast food, sub-prime financial services and gambling outlets – may encourage unhealthy behaviours in individuals and local communities, and this is an issue explored in Chapter 4.

Connectivity and accessibility
Connectivity has been a further focus of active travel studies. The premise is that the more *physically* connected a route network is – with shorter distances between junctions and

fewer dead-ends – the more conducive it is to active travel. This is based on the fact that connected networks provide a choice of quick and direct routes to get from one place to another. As with diversity and density, connectivity is important, although on its own it is not necessarily a good predictor of active travel.

A key issue is that you really cannot separate out connectivity from concepts of accessibility. For example, it does not matter how quick and direct a route is; people will not use it if they perceive it to be dangerous, or maybe just unpleasant and unwelcoming. Accessibility, therefore, is an issue that is both physical and psychological. Moreover, there are a myriad of factors which will contribute to whether people feel routes are suitable for use, and these will change with the perspective of the individual user. Those who lack confidence outside, or who have mobility or other impairments, such as sight loss, will also perceive environments differently; an issue we return to in the final chapter, when we discuss 'universality' versus 'plurality' in design.

Distance
A pivotal factor of urban form that influences active travel decisions is, naturally, distance. Generally, there is a strong inverse correlation between active travel and the distance between origin and destination. Many walkability studies use a 'rule of thumb' measure of 400 or 500 metres as a reasonable distance that most people will undertake on foot. This assumes a 5–10 minute walk, dependent on walking speed. However, this almost certainly underestimates the distance that most people find easy to walk. Research on 12 suburban areas of England found that 90 per cent of all journeys of less than 400 metres were carried out as active travel; however, so were just under 75 per cent of journeys of 400–800 metres (Sustrans, 2016). Research undertaken in Newcastle on how far people walked (Fig.3.5) again suggests that 800 metres might be a better measure of a reasonable distance, but that walking patterns also include hidden complexity.

In focus: how far will people walk?

↑
Figure 3.5
Participant plan – in 'How far do I walk?' study

Research carried out in Newcastle asked residents from various city locations to mark on a plan where they *regularly* walked to from home. The approximate distance and direction were then separately plotted. Figure 3.5 shows a fit and healthy person in their late sixties who regularly walked a distance of two kilometres (though the largely uphill return journey was by bus). While distances and frequency varied considerably between participants, the work concluded that the 400–500 metres often used as a 'reasonable walking distance' generally underestimates how far adults will walk, and that 700–800 metres might be a more realistic figure for the UK. The study also revealed that people's journeys often followed specific and limited routes from home – therefore walkability studies that consider an equidistant buffer (e.g., 500 metres) around individual's homes are not necessarily a good approximation of real life.

▬

Increasing active travel through intervention

If the basic components that support walking and cycling are known, this raises the possibility of increasing active travel by addressing deficiencies in the existing built environment. This is not straightforward, however, since not only are interventions in the built environment costly, but controlled experiments are very difficult to undertake. However, evidence does exist, for example, from projects carried out by the transport charity Sustrans (2016), particularly their Connect2 projects based in over 80 communities across the UK, which have created an invaluable body of 'natural experiments'.[1]

The Connect2 projects have shown that high-quality, traffic-free routes do increase overall physical activity levels in communities, with the greatest impact on those living close by (within one kilometre) and in households with no car. Moreover, people did not exercise less in other ways, meaning there was a significant overall increase in physical activity (Goodman et al., 2014). However, the picture on modal shift (using more active travel rather than motorised travel) is more complex. Here researchers suggested that 'passive exposure' – in other words, proximity alone– did not correlate with modal shift, leading the researchers to posit that infrastructure alone might not be enough to ensure that people shift their travel behaviours (Song et al., 2017). Broader research focusing on behaviour change also suggested that interventions were likely to be more successful when infrastructure change was supported with social programmes (Wilkie et al., 2018).

The six Cycling Demonstration Towns (2005–2011) and 12 Cycling Cities and Towns (2008–2011) in England also provide useful evidence. Initiatives included investment in both infrastructure – for example, cycle lanes, showers and cycle parking at workplaces – and supporting programmes (such as cycle training), fostering a 'cycle culture' among employees, and assisting employers with developing active travel plans. Across the 18 towns, overall cycling increased by approximately 1 per cent (there was also an increase in walking to work and a decrease in driving). Significantly, impacts were greatest in areas with highest deprivation. However, the study did note that there were considerable differences in impact at individual town level (Goodman et al., 2013).

A more recent study of London's 'mini-Holland' programme – part of Transport for London's 'Healthy Streets' initiative (Transport for London/Mayor of London, 2017) – has also had encouraging results (Fig.3.6).

In focus: London's mini-Holland schemes

↑
Figure 3.6
Mini-Holland scheme, Orford Road, Walthamstow

The mini-Holland scheme in London's outer boroughs is creating pedestrian- and cycling-friendly streets. A longitudinal study compared data from 1,712 individuals sampled from households in mini-Holland boroughs and from similar outer boroughs with no interventions. The study found significant increases in active travel in those areas where substantial changes had been made (Aldred, Croft and Goodman, 2019).

Conclusions

1 *Car dependency*   Car-dependent travel leads to congestion, pollution and less physical activity, which in turn impose heavy direct and indirect costs on the health of individuals and communities.
2 *Current UK plans*   In the UK there are initiatives to reduce petrol and diesel car use, especially for more polluting

vehicles. However, while positive, Low Emission Zones (and similar policies) and switching to electric vehicles will have limited impact on health.

3 *Active travel*   Switching to more active travel (walking and cycling) is the most important issue. We know the basic dynamics involved in active travel – density, land-use diversity, design and distance. We also know that building high-quality, traffic-free networks in urban areas means that people use them and increase their physical activity.

A modal shift away from private cars to active transport is complex and requires a range of approaches, both social and economic. However, urban design and planning make an important contribution to the design of supportive environments.

Further reading

Nieuwenhuijsen, M. and H. Khries (eds) (2019). *Integrating Human Health into Urban and Transport Planning: A Framework*. Cham: Springer.

Pooley, C. (2013). *Promoting Walking and Cycling*. Bristol: Policy Press.

Pucher, J. and R. Buehler (2012). *City Cycling*. Cambridge, MA: MIT Press.

Chapter 4   **The Need for Healthy Homes and High Streets**

In this chapter we explore two key building blocks of healthy communities – housing and local shops – and examine why, and how, health impacts need to be addressed.

Introduction

As stated in Chapter 1, over a century ago the links between poor housing conditions and ill-health were firmly established, and it was a concern for those harmful conditions that led directly to the development of both public health legislation and modern planning. In recent decades, a number of parallel, yet interconnected, issues with UK housing have emerged. These problems are arguably less deadly than the insanitary conditions of the 19th century, yet they are, in many ways, also less straightforward to resolve.

Outside the home environment, there have also been seismic shifts in the nature and offer of local shopping areas. In many neighbourhoods, local shopping streets, which would have comprised a variety of retailers and a source of fresh foodstuffs, have become dominated by shops and services that are in various ways far from healthy, such as fast-food outlets and betting shops.

The home and its immediate environs should provide a safe and healthy place to live, and yet for many people this is far from the case. What are the problems, in detail, and how might we begin to address them?

—

Housing issues

People spend a significant time in and around their homes. Home should be a place where people feel safe, secure and welcome. Homes should contribute positively to mental and physical health. Overall, housing[1] conditions have improved in the UK in recent decades. However, the *English Housing Survey 2019 to 2020* (MHCLG, 2020a) highlights that, nevertheless, 12 per cent of dwellings in the social rented sector, 23 per cent in the privately rented sector, and 16 per cent of owner-occupied homes do not meet the current Decent Homes Standard[2] (DCLG, 2006).

While urban designers and planners do not necessarily get involved in the interior planning and maintenance of housing, it is important to understand the health implications of poor-quality stock. Moreover, many people living in inadequate housing conditions are likely to experience problems in and around their neighbourhood, and it is therefore important to appreciate the ways in which these multiple issues can interact and exacerbate health impacts.

Living conditions in the home

The health and well-being of those who live in poor housing conditions can be severely impaired – both directly and indirectly (Fig.4.1). Damp, cold and mould are associated with respiratory and cardiovascular problems and increased communicable disease transmission. Noise, due to poor soundproofing, is further linked to lack of sleep, anxiety, depression and overall poor mental health. Often poor-quality housing will exhibit multiple problems, which may include trip and fall hazards due to badly maintained stairs and flooring and/or poor lighting. Fire risks are associated with poorly maintained wiring and lack of working fire alarms. Many of these issues can be addressed though improving thermal/noise performance and routine repair and maintenance. Research has shown that routine home upgrading can reduce hospital admissions, particularly for vulnerable groups (Hollinghurst et al., 2020).

Overcrowding and/or living in cramped conditions are significant issues for individuals' well-being, and it is estimated

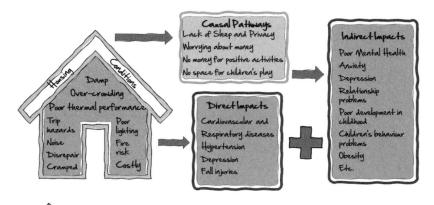

↑
Figure 4.1
Direct and indirect impacts of poor housing

that currently around 3.7 million people in the UK live in cramped homes (National Housing Federation, 2020). Moreover, 9 per cent of renters in social housing and 7 per cent of renters in the private sector live in officially 'overcrowded' homes (meaning there are too many people for the number of rooms available). Overcrowding is also most acutely experienced in minority ethnicity households (Wilson and Barton, 2013).

Surveys of inadequate space and overcrowding in UK homes suggest that around 30 per cent of respondents have suffered mental and/or physical impacts. Children living in cramped and overcrowded homes are particularly vulnerable and are likely to suffer poor physical and mental health, display behaviour problems and under-achieve at school (Shelter, 2006). However, inadequate interior space is only part of the issue: as again highlighted during the lockdown period of the COVID-19 crisis, many homes lack useable outdoor space as well, compounding issues for these residents.

Cost and affordability of housing
Housing costs in the UK have increased significantly over the past decade, and in 2020 an average home in England cost

approximately eight times the average annual salary, making this an unaffordable option for many. This has led to an increase in recent years in those living in the private rented sector where – as outlined above – the poorest housing conditions are found. Housing costs in the rented sector on average also account for one-third of income – compared to less than one-fifth for those with mortgages – making renting a relatively expensive option compared to home ownership (MHCLG, 2020b). Social housing is more affordable, but demand considerably outstrips supply.

Being worried about housing affordability has been highlighted as a contributor to poor mental health (Shelter, 2017), and is also linked to high blood pressure, hypertension and depression (Marí-Dell'Olmo et al., 2017). Moreover spending high proportions of income on housing can leave too little left to pay for healthy lifestyle options, such as buying nutritious food or taking part in leisure-time activities. Affordability and overcrowding are also inter-linked, as households may be tempted to share space with others to try to make ends meet, ending up with inadequate space for all involved.

Fuel poverty
Fuel poverty is a particular affordability issue associated with housing costs. Currently, the UK government defines someone as living in fuel poverty when, after spending the required amount to heat their home, they are left with a residual income below the official poverty line. According to official figures, fuel poverty has been slowly decreasing, yet around 10 per cent of homes are still classified as fuel-poor (Gov.UK, 2021). The impacts are particularly serious for frail, older people, who are vulnerable to hypothermia and communicable winter illnesses, and children, who may develop life-long asthma from exposure to damp and mould. However, fuel poverty can also lead to social isolation as some people effectively retreat to a single, heatable room in their home, which can lead to social isolation, poor mental health and increased risk of developing dementia.

New homes: a continuing problem
While new homes are unlikely to display problems of damp
and cold, problems of affordability and overall quality abound.
These issues were highlighted by a housing design audit of new
homes built by volume housebuilders[3] which was published
in 2020 (Place Alliance/CPRE, 2020). The audit found that
the design of 75 per cent of schemes audited was poor, or
mediocre, and one in five were so flawed that they should not
have been granted planning permission (Place Alliance/CPRE,
2020). New housing is much less affordable than existing
stock in many regions in the UK, and this is particularly true in
poorer regions (ONS, 2020). As noted previously, the impacts
of affordability are both direct and indirect, while the impacts
of poor design are multifactorial.

**In focus: car-orientated urban extension –
Great Park, Newcastle**

↑
Figure 4.2
Car-orientated urban extension

Housing built on former green belt land at Newcastle's Great Park arguably fails on many counts. Not only does the scheme lack local facilities, but large areas of public space – such as shown above – are dominated by roads and car parking. These neither support walking as a mode of transport, nor do they encourage social interaction (key to building a sense of community, reducing incidence of social isolation, etc.). Moreover, the generic design of the houses themselves is unlikely to create a sense of place in the future.

Unacceptable new design

The *Housing Design Audit* 2020 (Place Alliance/CPRE, 2020) did not specifically link new housing to impacts on health and well-being, but highlighted a series of pertinent issues. For example, few new developments were assessed as 'walkable' (see Chapter 3) (Fig.4.2); most lacked local facilities; and poorer areas were delivered the least inspiring designs – a possible source of future stigmatisation. Overall, most schemes lacked the characteristics that over time might help create a sense of place and belonging.

Office to residential conversion – a cause for real concern

A quite separate issue relating to housing has also been highlighted in recent research and this is the conversion of former office blocks to residential units. Spurred by housing shortages and relaxation of planning regulations – many office-to-residential conversions are 'permitted development'[4] – in some high demand areas as many as 75 per cent of new homes have come from these developments in the past few years, but serious concerns have been raised about the quality of many of these projects.

Converted blocks are often adjacent to busy roads and as such are exposed to high pollution levels. Few schemes offer usable green space, and almost none even have outside space by way of balconies. Furthermore, natural light is often restricted, and space standards are woefully poor. While the government's own guidance (MHCLG, 2015) suggests a minimum internal floor area of 37 square metres for a single-person studio or apartment, many conversions are barely one third of this size, and some are as small as just over 8 square metres (Levitt Bernstein, 2019). While the longer-term health consequences of living in these blocks has yet to be assessed – permitted development for this type of conversion has only been in place since 2013 (made permanent in 2016) – they will undoubtedly feature prominently in future research.

In focus: office-to-residential conversion – Newbury House, Redbridge, Ilford

Highlighted by a report on office-to-residential permitted development rights by architects Levitt Bernstein, the flats in Newbury House were highlighted as having a number of issues liable to impact health and well-being. Some flats face north and never receive direct sunlight; there are no balconies, or shared amenity space; and the location is adjacent to the A12 – a busy, polluted, dual carriageway.

Healthy, socially and economically diverse neighbourhoods

Beyond creating healthy, safe homes for the future, it is important to consider how these are grouped together to create 'neighbourhoods'. In Chapter 3, West Jesmond was highlighted as a late 19th-century 'walkable' neighbourhood with plenty of amenities. Today, this is a desirable inner suburb, but from the outset a range of home types were available, from large town-houses on leafier streets to rows of smaller terraced flats. This allowed people from different backgrounds to live alongside one another. Today, while prosperous, the area still houses a range of residents including students, families and retirees.

Unfortunately, too often today housing is built in mono-cultural swathes, offering no more choice than three- or four-bedroom variants of standard house types. It is generally aimed at a very narrow range of purchaser, and where social housing is incorporated, it is tucked away into less desirable plots. Sometimes there are visible differences between units that have been built for rent and those built for sale.

There have been attempts to argue that such social segregation is 'healthy', and that when people live alongside those who are similar to themselves it reduces stress (Halpern, 1995). However, this line of argument fails to consider that while living in socially segregated neighbourhoods *may* benefit some, it often harms the less well-off and exacerbates health inequalities. More broadly, for democratic societies to function, people need to interact with those from different walks of life, and counter-arguments to social segregation within neighbourhoods are far more compelling.

Social mixing can be designed into new places and work well, but this requires a level of care. In her study of new mixed developments Marion Roberts proposed four key characteristics for successful integration of tenures (Roberts, 2007).

- Potential visual differences; stigma must be avoided at all costs.
- A high-quality public realm where residents might encounter each other is essential.
- Where micro-districts (in other words, blocks) of different tenure are created, those different tenures need to share communal spaces.
- Density and height of developments must directly relate to a high-quality public realm to encourage use.

Despite these requirements seeming relatively deliverable and involving more 'care' than 'cost', the number of really successful mixed new neighbourhoods in the UK remains limited, though there are exceptions (Fig.4.3).

In focus: Branch Place, Colville Estate, Haringey – tenure-blind housing

↑
Figure 4.3
Branch Place, Colville Estate, Haringey

Branch Place is a sustainable mixed-tenure neighbourhood of 116 homes (60 per cent social rent, 10 per cent shared ownership, 30 per cent private sale), new public realm and playable landscaping and community growing areas in Hackney. The project provides the first replacement homes in the second phase of the Colville Estate Masterplan designed by Karakusevic Carson Architects. The design approach for Branch Place was established according to the principles set out in the Colville Estate Masterplan, the associated Design Code and Residents Charter, to ensure that the quality and designs defined by the community were locked into the project. Importantly, all homes were designed to be tenure-blind, with locally affordable housing, homes for social rent and those for market sale blended through the scheme and crafted with the same materials and finishes.

Healthy homes for the future

Clearly, many of the issues inherent in housing that impact health and well-being – particularly those relating to internal conditions – lie outside the realm of influence of urban designers and planners. However, awareness of these issues allows poor design to be challenged. Generally, in all aspects of design, 'quick-fix' solutions – of the type that office-to-residential use permitted development currently represents – are unlikely to produce satisfactory (and well-being-enhancing) environments; and this is a key message for all involved in housing development and delivery.

Overarching aspects of residential design that urban designers and planners can focus on with health outcomes in mind are as follows:

- *Physically greener environments* – around homes both private and public. This issue is explored in detail in Chapter 5. However, in essence, useable greenspaces are essential for physical and mental health, and even views out onto landscaping can assist mental restoration.
- *Walkable communities* – as set out in Chapter 3. If people are going to be enabled to be physically active in their day-to-day lives, that activity has to be 'designed in' from the outset.
- *Socially diverse communities* – to avoid social segregation and the associated negative impacts on health inequalities. Create shared spaces for social interaction and for a sense of social cohesion to develop, as outlined above.
- *Design quality* – greater attention to design quality at all scales and during all stages in the design process should underpin all of the above dimensions. Importantly, achieving this should not add to the cost of housing development (and thereby exacerbate affordability issues).

A note on 'design codes'

Widespread adoption of design codes – sets of detailed principles to guide development – could be a significant step forward in ensuring greater quality in residential design and *could* ensure that health and well-being are as much as possible 'designed in' to future development. Design codes are not new and regulations about design (encompassing appearance as well as structural performance) have existed in many countries and in many forms for centuries, ensuring visual harmony, as well as build quality in line with the standards of the day. However, in more recent decades the adoption of design codes in New Urbanist[5] settlements in the US has attracted much attention. There have also been recent successful examples in the UK (see the overview of Oakfield, Swindon, in Chapter 7); however, their adoption in this country has remained limited.

After a long campaign by urban designers in the UK (met with inaction by successive governments), the Ministry of Housing, Communities and Local Government (MHCLG) launched a National Model Design Code in 2021. The code is effectively a 'how to' guide for local authorities; and although it is a guidance, not a policy document, prepared by local authorities in line with the Model Design Code, it should have weight within the wider planning system. However, while health/well-being is mentioned, the document lacks detail in this respect. Therefore, whether the guide will bring forward healthier housing schemes remains unclear.

—

High streets: a changing shopping offer

Outside of the home, most urban neighbourhoods from the late 19th century until the 1960s would be provided with a range of local shops, and often a larger 'high street' area would be within easy – that is, walkable – reach. However, during the 1960s, significant transformations in retailing and related shopping habits began to take hold. Small independent retailers began to be replaced by self-service 'chains'. This trend spread into all retail sectors to the extent that by the start of the 21st century, the term 'clone towns' had been coined as a somewhat pejorative reflection on the lack of diversity in many shopping areas across the country (Conisbee et al., 2005).

A further development in the 1980s – boosted by favourable planning and financial policies – was the advent of 'out of town' shopping. Retailers (re)located to large, bespoke, shopping malls serviced with ample free parking (often in direct competition with existing centres). This development was seen to signal a change, whereby the formerly largely mundane undertaking of 'going shopping' now became viewed as a leisure activity. Malls became 'destinations', featuring entertainment facilities such as cinemas and bowling alleys. Finally, over the past decade there has been a significant switch to online retailing – a trend accelerated by the COVID-19 crisis, which effectively forced many consumers to shop this way who may not have considered doing so before.

The cumulative impact on town and city centres has been dramatic. During the past century, centres have witnessed the boom and then disappearance of many 'big name' companies – ones which had featured prominently in UK retailing for decades (Fig.4.4). Now, many city centres suffer from an oversupply

↑
Figure 4.4
Many well-known 'names' have disappeared from shopping centres
leaving large amounts of empty retail space

of retail space and these will need judicious reinvention going forward. However, arguably it is in secondary, neighbourhood 'high streets' that the most significant impacts on community health and well-being have occurred, and it is to these that we now turn.

—

Toxic high streets

As suggested in Chapter 3, having a diverse range of shops and other facilities close to home is associated with higher levels of active travel. However, in some neighbourhoods it is the nature of access and availability to local shops and services which is of concern. In many poorer communities, shopping parades that would once have comprised grocers, butchers, bakers, and so on, have become dominated by outlets and services which are *potentially* unhealthy and which bombard the shopper with tempting offers (Fig.4.5). These locations also often exude an air of neglect, with graffitied security shutters, litter-strewn pavements, congestion and high pollution levels. The term 'toxic high streets' has been coined by the author to encapsulate this phenomenon (Townshend, 2017).

↑
Figure 4.5
Toxic high streets – tempting offers?

Underpinning the concept of toxic high streets: 'obesogenic environments' and 'syndemics'

The concept of toxic high streets draws on two broader ideas from the field of public health. Firstly, 'obesogenic environments', a term coined by Swinburn and Egger (2002) to represent the accumulation of influences in people's lives and their surrounding environments that promote obesity in individuals and populations. Today, obesogenic – obesity-promoting – environments are perceived to be the driving force behind the current global obesity pandemic (Lake and Townshend, 2006).

The second underpinning concept is that of 'syndemics' – these are the aggregation of two or more concurrent disease clusters in a community with biological interactions, which exacerbate the prognosis and burden of those individual diseases. This term was developed in the 1990s (see Singer and Clair (2003).

Many poorer communities are exposed, first, to risk from obesity and related health harms, but *also* concurrently a range of other issues, such as indebtedness and addiction, exacerbated by ready access, availability and promotion of certain services on local high streets. Research aiming to establish the interconnectedness of health and well-being risks of these combinations of shops and services is ongoing. However, as outlined below, the individual risks are largely already established.

Takeaway fast food

One of the largest changes to traditional high street areas in the recent past has been the expansion of outlets selling takeaway food. While specific foodstuffs cannot be labelled 'obesogenic', nutritionists have established which foods are most implicated in excess weight gain and obesity. These are energy-dense, nutritionally poor and contain high quantities of fat, salt and sugar (Lake, Townshend and Burgoine, 2017). Such foods comprise the majority of offer in hot food takeaways (HFTs) where they are often served in excessively large portions; thus, regular consumption of these can lead to unhealthy weight gain.

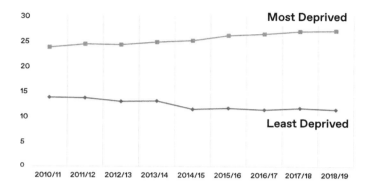

↑
Figure 4.6
Obesity rates in children from least and most deprived areas

Secondary school-aged children are particularly at risk of over-consumption when they acquire some independence over food purchase. HFTs also cluster in areas of deprivation, and exposure in poorer areas can be five times higher than in more affluent ones (Townshend and Lake, 2017). People from poorer socio-economic status (SES) backgrounds are more likely to over-consume HFTs, and although the reasons behind this are not entirely clear, this renders these communities highly susceptible to health consequences (Burgoine et al., 2016). Of concern is that, while overall childhood obesity rates in England have remained steady (if too high) over the past few years, the gap in rates between children in poor and affluent communities has steadily widened. Children in poorer areas are now more than twice as likely to be overweight, or obese, than their affluent counterparts (NHS Digital, 2020) (Fig.4.6).

HFTs may not only be bad for physical health. They are also associated with increased litter and anti-social behaviour, and when premises are closed and shuttered, they convey a general appearance of neighbourhood neglect. It is likely that these negative aspects add to the burden of stress and poor mental health in disadvantaged communities. However, this is an issue which, to date, has been little researched.

Betting shops

The visibility of betting shops on high streets is another significant change in recent decades. In the 1960s, when gambling outlets were first officially sanctioned in the UK, they were located away from public gaze on side streets, where rents and rates were cheap. This changed in the 1970s when independent betting shops, or 'bookies', declined and 'chain' operators became the norm (reflecting wider changes in retailing). The gambling industry also sought to recast betting as 'entertainment', and smarter premises offering complimentary services – seating, refreshments, and so on – began to appear in more prominent locations (Jones, Hillier and Turner, 1994).

Betting, in its own right, is not inherently unhealthy when controlled and within the financial means of participants. However, gambling can become habitual – and problematic – for some people, with significant associated health risks such as susceptibility to substance abuse and psychiatric disorders (Thomas et al., 2010). Of concern, research has suggested that accessibility to gambling opportunities is a key factor in encouraging problematic gambling. Moreover, betting shops have clustered in low-income areas (Jones, Hillier and Turner, 1994; Thomas et al., 2010; Harman, 2011; Haringey Council, 2011) – in other words, communities where some people are already likely to be experiencing poor mental health, stress, poverty and indebtedness.

As with HFTs, betting shops have indirect as well as direct health and well-being consequences, and their presence has been linked to anti-social behaviour and petty crime (Harman, 2011; Haringey Council, 2011; Newham Council, 2016).

Moreover, they can have a negative impact on shopping streets as they present a 'dead' frontage – in other words, there is little interaction between the interior and the street outside

– and may also act as a discouragement to more vibrant uses locating near them.

Sub-prime finance and high-cost credit

Many poorer neighbourhoods in the UK have also witnessed the withdrawal of mainstream banking, as institutions streamline their provision and increasing proportions of customers and businesses switch to online services. Moreover, while pawnbrokers (where a loan is secured against an item of value) have always been present in poorer neighbourhoods, more recently there has been a burgeoning of 'payday' loan and 'rent-to-own' shops charging rates of interest that far exceed those of mainstream credit providers.

People with poor 'financial literacy' – those who find it difficult to understand basic financial matters – are particularly susceptible to taking out payday-type loans (Townshend, 2017). Although a cap was introduced in 2015 that means interest must not exceed 0.8 per cent per day and the total cost of the loan must not exceed 100 per cent of the amount borrowed, these rates mean borrowers still get into difficulties. Increased exposure to, and accessibility of, these services adds pressure to take out multiple loans – either consecutively or simultaneously (Townshend, 2017) – and in extreme circumstances people fall prey to illegal loan sharks. Again, as with problematic gambling, indebtedness adds to the overall burden of poor mental health in poorer communities.

Encouragingly, the number of payday loan shops has decreased since the 2015 imposition of interest caps (and the rent-to-own retail sector also appears to be losing some popularity). However, such services remain a concern in the most deprived communities.

Other less healthy shops and services

In addition to payday loan shops, betting shops and HFTs there are a number of other outlets which provide less than healthy offers, such as tanning salons. Shops selling cut-price (sometimes counterfeit) alcohol and cigarettes are also an issue.

Moreover, while traditional off-licences have declined steadily in the past decade (mostly as a result of being undercut on price by supermarkets), corner – or 'convenience' – stores often include quite substantial displays of alcoholic drinks, along with confectionery, sugary soft drinks, salty snacks and even hot food 'to go'. Some stores sell little, if anything, of nutritional value, often include eye-catching promotions for multiple buys, and in some respects are arguably more problematic in terms of 'food' offer than many HFTs.

Approaching healthy high streets

While there are some positive trends – for example, the reduction of sub-prime financial services – the state of many high streets remains precarious, and essentially what is on offer represents a risk rather than an asset for the health of neighbouring communities. There are, however, no 'quick fixes', and as outlined at the beginning of this section, the decline of local shopping areas has had a long trajectory and is multifactorial in nature. Much of the change in consumer habits lies outside of the boundaries of urban design and planning, but there are contributions to be made from the profession, as in the examples that now follow.

Interdisciplinary approaches and aligning public policies

Evidence suggests that aligning health policies across disciplines and local government departments is vital to their success (Carmichael et al., 2019). Since around 2009/10, local planning authorities have been introducing policies to prevent the further proliferation of HFTs; an excellent example of this is Gateshead's Supplementary Planning Document (Gateshead Council, 2015) which prevents further HFT uses in any ward which does not meet the authority's childhood obesity targets – in effect imposing a blanket ban. The policy was constructed by planning officers working closely in conjunction with their public health and environmental health colleagues – the former to provide the evidence base for links to local obesity rates, and the latter regularly working with food outlets to provide an informed insight into HFT operation throughout the borough. The guidance has been successfully defended at planning appeals and no HFTs have been granted planning permission in the borough since its adoption.

There are different planning approaches to HFT restriction:

- *Exclusion zones* – for example, around schools and children's centres.
- *Anti-clustering policies* – restricting the number of HFTs in a row, or percentage, of shop frontages.
- *Location restriction* – only allowing new HFTs in certain shopping areas (for a fuller analysis, see Lake, Townshend and Burgoine, 2017).

However, some local authorities have also enacted wider, non-planning approaches in parallel – for example, Essex's 'Tuck-In Scheme' (Essex Tuck-In, 2021), a county-wide scheme run by environmental health officers. The scheme works in parallel with aims set out in the Essex Design Guide to promote access to healthier food. The key aims are to reduce portion sizes and reformulate recipes to make them healthier, by reducing salt, fat and sugar. While improving the healthfulness of the food offer is at the heart of the project, avoiding terminology about 'healthy diets' and advice that sounds too hectoring is seen as key to the scheme's success. The scheme – and similar ones in other authorities – provides examples of how to work *with* commercial providers. As a model it may be able to inspire approaches in other sectors that affect people's health – however, this requires more research.

Supporting communities who want change

Another approach is that of urban designers and planners working with communities who want change, or are resisting unhealthy development, by providing assistance, expertise and inspiration. There have been a number of campaigns countrywide – for example, the 'Stop the Whoppa' campaign in Newcastle's West End (Stop the Whoppa, 2020).

In focus: community actions to stop a 'drive-through' burger chain

More communities are trying to resist the spread of unhealthy development. The 'Stop the Whoppa' campaign in Newcastle's West End (Stop the Whoppa, 2020) is fighting a proposal for a drive-through restaurant on a former police station site, located opposite a school and nearby to a hospital complex which includes Newcastle University's Campus for Ageing and Vitality. One of the noteworthy aspects of this grassroots campaign is that it is located in Newcastle's Elswick ward. Elswick is in the top 1 per cent of England's most deprived areas (using current indices of Multiple Indices of Deprivation), and members of the community seem unimpressed about the potential investment (as promoted by the developer) and much more concerned about the community. (See https://stopthewoppa.co.uk/)

Creative visions and interventions to support independent retail
Further, creative solutions that contribute positively to local shopping areas may not necessarily solve the deep-rooted problems faced by poorer areas, but can nevertheless provide inspiration for thinking 'outside the box' and provide further engagement opportunities for urban designers and planners. In Chapter 7, London's Wild West End project is reviewed as a commercially viable greening project, which shows what can be achieved from partnership working. Several London shopping areas are also providing free and safe cycle parking in empty shop units, an idea that might be adapted for more widespread use. In Newcastle, the removal of traffic from parts of the city centre, accompanied by temporary landscaping at weekends (first trialled in 2019 and re-introduced in summer 2021) – while controversial (as all road closures are) – has proved popular with families, creating a fun reason to visit (Fig.4.7).

Creating opportunities for local businesses to (re)establish themselves is also vital. During the COVID-19 crisis, business rate relief and other financial packages have enabled smaller local businesses to set up and thrive in the most unlikely of circumstances – lessons might be learned from analysing the dynamics of such examples (Fig.4.8), as well as giving pointers for how they might be supported into the future.

↑
Figure 4.7
A road closure for a pop-up landscape in Newcastle – while controversial –
proved popular (even on a damp morning!)

↑
Figure 4.8
A queue forms early for a bakery – an unexpected impact of COVID-19
has been the boom in buying local

Conclusions

Healthy homes

1 Home should be a place of sanctuary, a place of physical and mental well-being – not just a place to live, but a place to flourish. However, far too many UK homes fall short of this ideal.
2 While modern homes are better insulated and cheaper to run than older ones, affordability is a huge issue. Quick-fix solutions – such as converting former office accommodation – are unlikely to provide satisfactory homes, and the housing sector needs a substantive overhaul.
3 Furthermore, potential new 'neighbourhoods' that are being created need much greater care in their design. Bland swathes of mono-cultural housing are never going to develop a sense of place or vibrant, socially diverse, communities.

Healthy high streets

1 There has been a long and sustained decline in the healthfulness of offer from neighbourhood shopping streets, particularly in poorer communities.
2 The cumulative impact of unhealthy shops and services in poorer communities is undoubtedly exacerbating health inequalities.
3 There are no magic bullet solutions to resolving the issues of unhealthy high streets, but as with other aspects of creating healthier cities, interdisciplinary working and cooperation across private and public sectors will be key to any future success.

Further reading

Place Alliance and CPRE (2020). *A Housing Design Audit for England*. London: Place Alliance, http://placealliance.org.uk/research/national-housing-audit/

Royal Society for Public Health (2018). 'Health on the High Street: Running on Empty 2018', https://www.rsph.org.uk/our-work/campaigns/health-on-the-high-street/2018.html

**Green Infrastructure for Health
and Well-being**

In this chapter, we explore the essential benefits that vegetation, waterbodies and their associated wildlife provide for the health and well-being of urban dwellers.

Introduction

There is a burgeoning body of literature researching the benefits bestowed to humans by interacting with 'nature' in cities. This body of work has emerged from several disciplinary backgrounds including environmental psychology, landscape architecture and human geography. One of the issues with drawing on a large and diverse evidence base is that, inevitably, terminology is used differently from study to study. 'Greenspace' and 'green infrastructure', for example, are widely and variously utilised. 'Greenspace', in particular, is a loose term, but in this chapter it will refer to open areas which are predominantly given over to vegetation and accessible for public use, such as parks and recreation grounds.

'Green infrastructure', usually denoted by the acronym 'GI', emerged in the mid-1990s. It also has numerous, subtly different, definitions offered by academic and non-academic sources. The UK government, for example, suggests that GI embraces a network of all spaces and assets that provide environmental and wider benefits. This includes larger public and private areas such as parks and urban woodlands, smaller spaces, including private gardens, and features such as street trees and green roofs. It also encompasses all 'blue' elements, such as canals, sustainable drainage systems, streams and ponds (Gov.UK, 2016). The term further implies an approach to the strategic planning of *all* assets to promote associated social, economic and environmental benefits. This is a relatively simple, yet all-encompassing, definition and will be adopted for this chapter.

Human needs: from 'prospect-refuge' to 'affordances'

For hundreds of thousands of years, humans led a hunter-gatherer existence in a truly natural environment. To survive, it was necessary to understand and interact with that natural world. Today, we might consider ourselves sophisticated, urban, tech-savvy, or whatever term we choose to separate ourselves *out* from nature. However, in reality, we are still part of it. Moreover, some of our primordial instincts still influence our behaviour, whether we are aware of them or not. In addition, the COVID crisis has highlighted people's inherent need for contact with 'nature' (Fig.5.1).

↑
Figure 5.1
A community 'garden' created (illegally) on a back lane pavement as soon as the COVID-19 lockdown was eased

Appleton's prospect-refuge theory (Appleton, 1975) is a useful departure point to explore these issues. Appleton observed animal behaviour to develop his 'habitat theory'. He proposed that humans have innate preferences to landscape types which reflect their basic instincts to survive. People, he suggests, are drawn to places that provide 'prospect' (especially the ability to see danger coming), while at the same offering protection from being seen, or 'refuge'. We can still observe this behaviour, for example, in the study of locations chosen by teenagers to 'hang out' in parks (Townshend and Roberts, 2013).

On a more expansive note, the biophilia hypothesis (Wilson, 1984) also focuses on instinctive behaviours that are rooted in the evolutionary origins of humans. Biophilia theory suggests that humans are attracted to places that indicate sources of food, fresh water and shelter. Urban parks, with their ornamental lakes and planting schemes, in essence replicate some of these features, albeit in a limited way; theoretically, however, they are sufficient to satisfy those evolutionary impulses.

A further useful concept for urban planners and designers, is that of 'affordances', developed by Gibson (1979). Affordances, he posits, are what environments offer animals (including humans) for their own use. Affordances suggest possible actions, and people perceive those possibilities without the need for mental calculation – although whether they act on the offer is a matter of personal choice. Affordances, therefore, provide a baseline theory for understanding how and what behaviours are supported by certain environments. Of importance, GI provides a multitude of affordances, especially for children, who are spontaneous in their actions. For example, a tree might offer them something to run round, hide behind, climb up, swing from, or a host of other possibilities. However, even for adults, green spaces usually offer a rich and diverse range of passive and active engagement (Fig.5.2).

—

Restoring, facilitating and mitigating
Beyond reactions based on primordial instincts, various pathways have been proposed to explain the benefits that GI provides

↑
Figure 5.2
A sunny canal bank provides the perfect vantage area to observe
the 'pop-up' market on the opposite side

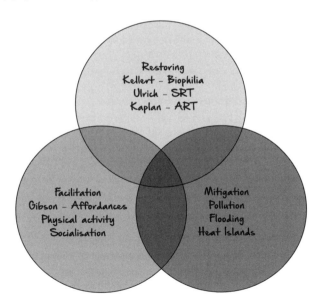

Restoring
Kellert – Biophilia
Ulrich – SRT
Kaplan – ART

Facilitation
Gibson – Affordances
Physical activity
Socialisation

Mitigation
Pollution
Flooding
Heat Islands

↑
Figure 5.3
The overlapping pathways between GI and well-being

in contemporary cities. Studies include both theoretical and empirical work and generally focus on specific themes, such as reducing or relieving harmful stress, providing opportunities for physical activity, offering space for social interaction, or improving air quality (Wilson, 1984). For urban planners and designers, I have found it useful to reframe these into three overarching spheres of 'restoring', 'facilitating' and 'mitigating'. However, it should be noted that these impacts are not discrete, but interrelated (Fig.5.3).

Restoring
The ability of GI to restore our mental well-being has received much attention. Two key theories have been proposed. The first was initially based on observations of hospital patient recovery. Ulrich noted that patients who had a view of nature recovered more quickly and took less analgesics than patients with no view. Ulrich's work proposes that there are processes deep within the brain which mean that views of natural environments block negative thoughts and emotions. This process induces a sense of calmness, reduces stress, and therefore aids recovery (Ulrich et al., 1991).

His work is sometimes therefore referred to as Stress Reduction Theory (SRT) and his findings have been replicated a number of times by other researchers. An interesting aspect of SRT is that *views* of natural environment appear to be sufficient to stimulate the beneficial processes involved. This is in contrast to most explanatory pathways linking GI and well-being, which involve some element of immersal in, or interaction with, GI.

It should be noted, of course, that stress is a natural process and in small doses is beneficial. When we sense our bodies are under threat, the body responds by releasing hormones which, for example, speed up reaction time and boost stamina – part of the so-called 'fight or flight' response. However, sustained stress over a long time – referred to as chronic stress – is dangerous and has been linked to a range of diseases and disorders, from poor mental health to heart disease. According to SRT, contact with more natural environments should help people cope with harmful levels of stress in day-to-day life. Evidence was found of this in a study of people living in poorer neighbourhoods in Scotland. Here, people living under stressful circumstances but in greener environments had lower levels of cortisol (the body's stress hormone) compared to equivalent individuals living in less green areas (Thompson et al., 2012).

A second pathway to mental well-being is proffered by Attention Restoration Theory (ART) (Kaplan, 1995). Contemporary lives generally require substantial and sustained attention to carry out day-to-day tasks – for example, driving to work, or using a computer when we get there. However, the human attention span is finite and too much focused attention can overload our sensory systems. This causes mental fatigue. Natural environments capture our attention in an effortless, non-stressful way – for example, when we notice a bee collecting nectar from a flower, or hear a bird singing. ART suggests that this allows us to rest our cognitive response systems and restore our mental capacities. There is also compelling evidence for ART. For example, attention has been shown to increase dramatically after a walk in a greenspace, but not after a walk in urban environments (Berman, Jonides and Kaplan, 2008), and even short exposure to views of green roofs are proven to boost mental faculties (Lee et al., 2015).

Most studies that have explored the restorative effects of GI have been based on SRT or ART, or a combination of both, and there is good evidence that the two processes may work in tandem. Studies have shown, for example, that exposure to GI is associated not only with positive mood enhancement, but with physiological reactions such as reduced blood pressure (Hartig et al., 2003; Pretty et al., 2005; Aspinall et al., 2015). More broadly, research has suggested lower all-cause mortality for those living nearer green areas, even when adjusted for socio-economic factors (Mitchell and Popham, 2008), and the benefits that it brings often go beyond what individual components might suggest possible (Science Advisory Council, 2019).

Water, stress and well-being

Studies of GI and stress often examine people's reaction to landscape images. These include waterbodies as part of the landscape; however, the specific influence of water is rarely examined on its own. We know people enjoy views of water, because, for example, residential properties offering these command a premium, and urban public spaces adjacent to water are highly prized, especially in fine weather (Fig.5.4). We also know that in specific surroundings water can have positive impacts on people's well-being, bringing into play visual, auditory and olfactory senses. These are often harnessed in 'healing gardens' at healthcare and other settings (Cooper Marcus and Sachs, 2014). Research also suggests that living near water – for example, the coast, lakes and/or rivers – also improves the mental health of individuals (Pasanen et al., 2019). There is, however, currently a lack of evidence relating to these impacts in relation to urban blue spaces.

↑
Figure 5.4
Urban waterbodies are perennially popular, as here in Dublin

It should be noted, however, that the presence of urban water is not always positive. The threat of too much water and flooding can be extremely stressful to communities. In flooding incidents, this includes individuals who have not been directly affected. Moreover, studies have also shown that the negative impacts from flooding events can persist over several generations and as such can be extremely challenging to overcome.

Facilitating sociability and physical activity

GI is excellent for facilitating sociability in neighbourhoods, and research suggests that greener neighbourhoods are generally perceived as more friendly. Parks and other open spaces not only provide destinations for pre-arranged get-togethers between friends, but are places where people are likely to bump into neighbours by chance. This in turn facilitates social 'cohesion' – or the extent to which people know and trust others living close by.

Greenspaces are particularly powerful for creating social cohesion because they are 'neutral' places. In other words, they do not require individuals to possess any specific beliefs, affiliations or interests to use them – unlike clubs, religious and other institutions. They are also relatively socially inclusive, being free to use, and they allow interaction between people from different backgrounds and ages. They are, therefore, helpful in combatting feelings of isolation for less mobile groups, such as older people. However, some individuals/groups may feel unwelcome in some spaces, and this must always be taken into consideration.

Parks and other greenspaces also provide safe, attractive settings for physical activity, essential to maintain healthy weight and combat lifestyle conditions and diseases as outlined in Chapter 2. There is good evidence that exercise performed in green settings is more beneficial than equivalent energy expended indoors, for example, by reducing blood pressure and increasing improvements to mood. Again, park-based physical activity is generally socially inclusive, often requiring little specialist equipment, and for children the affordances offered by parks stimulate extra physical effort. There is also strong evidence that links being physically active with positive mental health (Schuch et al., 2016). This suggests that in GI spaces physical activity, ART and SRT processes may well work in conjunction with each other to improve mental health.

If parks are excellent settings for physical activity, this does somewhat beg the question of whether their presence stimulates people to be more physically active than they otherwise would be. Here the evidence becomes a little more complex, and despite some studies showing links between living in close proximity to green spaces and being physically active, overall reviews have shown inconsistent results (Lachowycz and Jones, 2011; Bancroft et al., 2015). A key problem in comparing results is that these studies adopt a wide variety of measures and metrics, and many do not assess the *quality* of greenspace provided in enough detail.

Overall, however, the body of work suggests that proximity to facilities may not always engender use – and particularly in communities that feel disenfranchised, encouragement, for example, through social programmes, may be needed. In relation to quality, the presence of facilities such as age-appropriate play equipment is important and high standards of management and maintenance are also key issues. Research, however, has also suggested that physical activity levels increase with *greater* biodiversity.

Water and physical activity
Research in the UK has found a link between living near the coast and increased levels of physical activity, suggesting that in this case, proximity is a key driver to active engagement. Moreover, longitudinal research in Finland found that living close to useable waterbodies was associated with healthy weight management (Halonen et al., 2014). There may be possibilities to extend these benefits in urban areas. In Copenhagen, for example, swimming in specific areas of city centre waterways is encouraged, though this is not an approach adopted in the UK and there is no UK evidence relating to physical activity and proximity to urban waterbodies at present.

Mitigating

The final aspect of green-blue spaces that needs consideration is the mitigation of conditions that are in other ways damaging to health and well-being. There are four key issues: improving air pollution, reducing noise pollution – both of which, as outlined in Chapter 3, are often associated with road traffic – heat mitigation and flood risk alleviation.

Air pollution

There is a growing body of research exploring GI, reduced air pollution and improved air quality. GI, for example, generally produces little or no pollution itself. Therefore, at the city scale GI should reduce overall concentrations of pollutants. GI also absorbs the greenhouse gas carbon dioxide (CO_2) – this is sometimes referred to as a 'carbon sink'. Furthermore, some types of plants can remove other pollutants, for example, trees that trap PM on their leaves and bark. Some trees, such as Silver Birch (*Betula pendula*), are particularly good at this, and though there is significant variation between species, broadly speaking, deciduous trees are superior in this regard due to their larger leaf area.

Noise pollution

Similarly to air pollution (above), GI produces little noise, and indeed the 'natural' noises associated with it (such as birdsong) have potentially beneficial impacts (Annerstedt et al., 2013), so there is an attenuating effect on urban noise pollution due to its very existence. However, there is also good evidence that planting can act as an acoustic barrier, effectively blocking out unwanted noise. It does this by absorbing and/or interfering with sound waves. Furthermore, screening busy roads from residential areas can provide a psychological barrier, which also reduces the stress associated with traffic noise (Van Renterghem et al., 2013).

Heat reduction

Urban areas demonstrate a phenomenon known as the 'heat island' effect. Man-made structures and hard surfaces, such as concrete and asphalt, absorb and store solar energy to a greater extent than vegetation. In addition, waste heat generated by energy usage and slower wind speeds in built-up areas are secondary contributors. The result is an increase in air temperature in urban areas compared to the surrounding rural hinterland. In times of high temperatures, heat stored during the day in urban settings is then slowly released at night which prevents night-time cooling. In turn this can prevent people from recovering after day-time high heat exposure. Heat is an augmented risk for many people with underlying chronic conditions, and the effects can be fatal in vulnerable groups such as the elderly (Laaidi et al., 2012). This is of special concern as higher global temperatures – due to climate change and extreme weather events such as heat waves – become more likely.

GI mitigates the heat island through a process known as evapotranspiration – the process by which water is transferred from the land to the atmosphere by evaporation from the soil and by transpiration from plants. Also, shading from plants prevents ground surfaces from heating up as much as they otherwise would. Therefore, maximising the proportion of GI in cities – and this includes green walls, roofs and other surfaces – is an important strategy in heat island effect reduction. The situation with waterbodies may be complicated, however. While generally water is associated with cooling properties, and air temperature near moving water (rivers) has been shown to mitigate heat islands (Hathaway and Sharples, 2012), the static water in urban lakes may not have the same positive impact.

Flooding
Millions of homes in the UK are at risk of flooding, and the risks are increased by climate change and more extreme and unpredictable weather events. GI in urban areas is an essential element in flood mitigation, and wherever possible water-sensitive urban design (WSUD) should be employed. WSUD aims to promote holistic design that establishes greater harmony between communities and water. The key principle is to address the needs of the natural water cycle, yet at the same time create

places that are attractive, functional and valued by those who live and work there (Abbott et al., n.d). This includes sustainable urban drainage systems (SUDS), areas for ground percolation (absorption of water into the ground), new water bodies, reed beds, and so on. These features can be attractively designed to exploit the positive aspects of water for well-being, while alleviating flood risk and its attendant negative issues.

Urban allotments and community gardens

Urban allotments and community gardens are an element of GI which deserve special consideration in relation to well-being. Allotments tend to be divided up into individual (often sizeable) plots while community gardens, by their definition, are more communal. However, community gardens may allocate individual responsibility for certain areas, while allotment associations often have communal projects, such as creating wildlife areas in leftover spaces. Also, while traditional allotments are usually large in size, grouped together on considerable parcels of land and available to anyone to rent, new 'mini-allotments' have been integrated into developments, intended for local residents only. As such the boundaries between allotments and community gardens are blurred, and while they have different emphases, they have many benefits in common.

Gardening promotes beneficial outdoor physical exercise for adults of all ages, as well as promoting mental and spiritual well-being (Fig.5.5). Allotments can also provide a safe place for children's outdoor exercise. Additionally, while certain activities, such as digging, can be quite strenuous, gardens and plots can often be adapted to suit a person's physical abilities – for example, by using raised beds, which can be enjoyed by persons with reduced mobility. Moreover, while gardening generally requires a moderate level of mobility, activities are inclusive to those with visual and/or auditory impairment, for example, through sensory experiences of touch and smell. It is perhaps no surprise that gardening is successfully used as occupational

↑
Figure 5.5
Allotments – sites of physical activity, mental and spiritual well-being

therapy for recovery from a wide range of injuries, diseases and conditions, both physical and mental.

Gardening as an activity has been shown to improve mental health by reducing acute stress, depression and anger, and has been shown to improve self-esteem and confidence, and promote feelings of well-being (Townshend, 2016). These aspects can also help with recovery, by helping convalescents bond with others, feel valued and accepted as part of a social group and be functional in a setting where they can interact with members of the wider community. Some studies have also shown positive benefits to those suffering from dementia. These benefits clearly go beyond the more general restorative aspects of engagement with GI outlined at the beginning of the chapter.

Some of the above benefits are obviously also gained from gardening in a private garden; however, gardening as a social activity provides an additional sense of 'connectedness' that can strengthen sense of identity and belonging. Gardening has also been used as a way of reconnecting with hard-to-reach groups such as teenage offenders. Communal gardens can particularly bring different communities together, break down barriers, help combat social isolation and provide the basis for support mechanisms in times of need, by growing and sharing together. Studies of refugees, for example, have shown that gardening fosters social networks, helps to reaffirm identities – for example, by growing familiar foods – and aids in adaption to new circumstances (Gerodetti and Foster, 2016).

Allotments and community gardens can also reconnect urban dwellers with healthy food production, and having an allotment has been linked directly to improved diet and increased consumption of fruit and vegetables. Some community-based initiatives have picked up on this potential (Fig.5.6).

In focus: Incredible Edible Todmorden

↑
Figure 5.6
One of the many communal planting beds in Todmorden

Run by a small group of dedicated volunteers, Incredible Edible Todmorden began in 2007 by utilising the town's abandoned or unwanted areas of ground (such as a corner of the railway station car park) to grow herbs, vegetables and fruit that were free for anyone in the community to share. The venture is still entirely voluntary but has grown into a holistic local food campaign. The initiative has spawned a number of similar movements in towns across the UK and well beyond. (See https://www.incredible-edible-todmorden.co.uk/)

Urban forests and 'forest bathing'

The issue of urban forests is another aspect of GI that needs consideration. The concept of urban forests not only includes those areas of actual woodland found in and around urban areas (valuable as they are), but more broadly, all trees in parks and amenity areas, along transport routes such as canals, street trees and even those in domestic gardens. The importance of the concept has been highlighted in the recent past, because while there has been some notable increase in urban tree cover, in many UK cities, street trees which were planted in large numbers in the 19th century have undergone removal at an alarming rate. In Sheffield, for example, over 5,000 mature trees were removed in a five-year period, prompting huge controversy in the community.

As stated earlier, trees are particularly important for their impact on mitigating various forms of pollution, while native trees are important for biodiversity (discussed below). However, some research has suggested an added benefit of contact with trees, and particularly wooded areas, over other types of vegetation. Forest bathing, or 'Shinrin-yoku', is a concept that has become popular in Japan since the 1990s and literally means being immersed in a wooded area; and moreover being conscious of the surroundings – the quality of the air, complex scents, the light, the colours, and so on – as a way of combatting stress (Miyazaki and Motohashi, 1995). In a way, it is a targeted form of SRT and ART combined (Fig.5.7).

One of the key qualities identified in the special restorative power of woodlands is that they promote biodiversity. As

↑
Figure 5.7
An urban woodland walk – a perfect way of combatting stress

previously stated, physical activity in GI appears to be linked to biodiversity; however, the restorative powers of GI may also increase without physical activity as a mediating factor.

A note of caution is required, however, in relation to wooded areas, in that not everyone necessarily perceives them positively; this will obviously be more likely if they are poorly maintained and mistreated (for example, through vandalism, fly-tipping, and so on).

Biodiversity and rewilding

Biodiversity refers to the numbers of different species of plants and animals found in any particular area. GI is very diverse in nature: for example, even two public parks in one city may vary hugely in terms of their offer, not just for humans, but for other species. Some areas will encompass diverse flora and fauna in a vast array of habitats, while others may be much more restricted. As previously stated, some studies have noted that people appear to be more physically active in environments which have greater biodiversity, although the reasons why are not fully understood.

More broadly, some researchers have suggested a biodiversity hypothesis based on exposure as essential for human health. Exposure to a diverse range of micro-organisms (such as bacteria) is known to be essential for humans to develop healthy immune systems and protect themselves, for example, against allergies. Many useful microbes are associated with natural environments, soil, plants and water. Early exposure to these is important, and children who are exposed to nature develop greater microbial diversity and less sensitivity to certain allergies (Ruokolainen et al., 2015). In adults, a lack of sustained contact with a variety of natural environments could lead to a dysfunctional immune system and therefore leave someone vulnerable to various infectious and autoimmune disorders (Rook, Raison and Lowry, 2014).

'Rewilding' is a term that is most associated with the large-scale restoration of ecosystems, where nature can take care of itself. It seeks to reinstate natural processes by, for example, reintroducing species that may have been extinct for some considerable time. The term first started being used by grass-roots ecologists in the 1990s. More recently, however, consideration has been given to introducing more wildlife diversity in urban areas – in other words 'urban rewilding'. Schemes such as London's Wild West End (see Chapter 7) provide the potential for huge increases in biodiversity in city areas, and while the impact on human health has yet to be studied in detail, the foregoing discussion implies the likelihood of positive impacts.

Nature Based Solutions (NBS)

Over the last decade, a new term has entered debates around GI and this is 'nature-based solutions' (NBS). NBS are interventions that utilise, replicate or modify natural processes that are designed to address a range of social, economic and environmental issues. As such, NBS is an umbrella term that includes many types of GI project, such as restoring wetlands to aid flood management, or using GI to mitigate over-heating in urban areas. Most of the approaches discussed in this chapter would fall within the scope of NBS. However, most projects labelled NBS currently focus on *ecological* issues. Therefore, the extent to which NBS impact human health has less of a focus in research. It might be observed here that, as the appreciation of socio-ecological interdependencies evolves, it may become more standard for research to explore the co-benefits of natural interventions – that is, simultaneous benefits for the human and natural world – rather than seeing these, and researching them, as distinct. Examples are the Econets report by Natural England which looked at human and wildlife benefits of ecological networks (Natural England, 2015), and Glasgow's relaunched 'Stalled Spaces' programme (see Chapter 7).

Conclusions

That GI responds to human needs and is generally beneficial to health and well-being is beyond doubt. The key issues are:

1 *Complexity*   There are a number of complex pathways involved in bestowing GI benefits. Moreover, these pathways overlay one another and/or interact in synergetic ways, and in many cases the exact mechanisms at play have yet to be fully explained. Framing the evidence around overlapping themes of *restoring*, *facilitating* and *mitigating* is intended to help make sense of this complexity.

2 *Inequalities*   GI, and the *quality* of GI, is particularly important in relation to addressing health inequalities since

many of its benefits are free and their impact on poorer communities is proven.

3 *Beyond health*   It should also be noted that GI has value for people that goes beyond affective, cognitive, physiological and amenity benefits. This is in its provision of multi-sensory (beyond the standard five senses), dynamic (i.e., ever-changing) and holistic experiences that cannot always be reduced to their component parts. It is valued for the opportunity it allows for nature engagement, and also, in and of itself, as a source of wonder and inspiration.

The key take-home message for urban planners and designers is that we should be *designing in as much opportunity for nature and biodiversity in urban areas as possible* – and where achievable, *retrofitting our existing built environment* in the same manner.

——

Further reading

Coles, R. and Z. Milliman (2013). *Landscape, Well-Being and Environment*. London: Routledge.

Coutts, C. (2016). *Green Infrastructure and Public Health*. London: Routledge.

Mell, I. (2019). *Green Infrastructure Planning*. London: Lund Humphries.

Ward, C., P. Aspinall and S. Bell (2010). *Innovative Approaches to Researching Landscape and Health*. London: Routledge.

Chapter 6

The Benefits and Burdens of the Past: Heritage, Place and Well-being

In this chapter we explore the potential influences on well-being from living with the physical traces of the past – buildings, monuments, and so on – all around us. While often positive, and a possible focus of community identity and place attachment, we recognise that the past was often brutal, particularly for certain groups in society – a challenge that needs to be addressed.

Introduction

Cities are dynamic places, constantly in flux, and the passage of time is evident in the built environment all around us. The changes that occur day to day, season to season and over centuries are an essential, though often overlooked, aspect of urban design. Kevin Lynch, one of the most notable writers in the discipline, devoted an entire volume to the subject – asking: 'What time is this place?' (Lynch, 1972).[1] Lynch encourages urban designers to reflect on the rhythms of the city, the human perspective of time, and how this influences what we save for future generations, and what we destroy to make way for progress.

On a more personal level, part of self-awareness is our ability to reflect on experiences and learn from them. Our memories, therefore, are an essential element of our well-being. Places often evoke those memories: the park where we played with friends when young; the cinema where we saw our first film – even if the building has now been put to a quite different use. The city is a 'theatre of memory', as the historian Raphael Samuel (1994) puts it, against which our lives are individually and collectively played out.

However, while many memories are precious, some are also painful. Some we might prefer to erase; scenes we would happily confine to the wrecking ball. And yet the locations of unpleasant events for one person, or group, may be precisely those treasured by others. The past is a complex and contested place.

—

Valuing the past around us

Trying to unpack the influence that the past around us has on our well-being is a far from easy task. To begin with, the past is not simply a factual list of dates and events; it is a moveable feast, constantly open to interpretation and re-evaluation. This applies to the historic built environment and in our attitude to the places we inhabit. Victorian buildings, for example, while now treasured, were from the early to the mid-20th century generally disregarded. Perceived as over-decorated and oppressive, they were unappreciated, even loathed (Fig.6.1). Indeed, buildings from any era will generally go through a period after construction where they are viewed as unfashionable and regarded as having little value.

Buildings, monuments, parks, gardens and anything else in the built environment that manages to survive, for whatever reason, will be continually reassessed. If they are regarded as worthy, they may well be declared part of our 'heritage'. Buildings can be 'listed' as being of historic and/or architectural interest, and a similar scheme allows the registration of parks and gardens. Moreover, conservation area status can be used for whole areas deemed worthy of protection and enhancement, and currently England alone has over 10,000 such designations (Pendlebury and Brown, 2021). Such processes clearly show that *value* is attached to these buildings, places and spaces by society.

Might that value, therefore, be linked to our individual and collective sense of well-being? Certainly, the heritage lobby

↑
Figure 6.1
Midland Hotel, St Pancras, though now treasured, was for
many years threatened with demolition

has made this claim in the recent past. A number of reports and
articles focusing on well-being have been issued by Historic
England (HE) – the body tasked with protecting the nation's
historic environment (Fujiwara, Cornwall and Dolan, 2014;
Monckton and Reilly, 2018; Reilly, Nolan and Monckton, 2018).[2]
These documents focus on a number of different themes that
might be summarised as *engagement*, *healing* and *sense of place/*

place attachment/identity. In an ambitious agenda to promote well-being through its work, HE also claims that its benefits are supported by surveys, research and empirical projects (Chadwick [1842]2012). The next paragraphs explore each of these three heritage-focused well-being narratives.

Engagement

The fact that engaging with the past in a myriad of ways is extraordinarily popular is beyond doubt. Television programmes about valuing antiques and restoring family treasures abound. Terms such as 'vintage', 'retro' and 'pre-loved' are used to describe what would at one time have simply been regarded as 'old' or 'second-hand'. Heritage attractions, from country houses to living museums, enjoy seemingly endless popularity. More generally, protecting historic buildings is widely supported, and conservation area legislation is one of the most successful aspects of contemporary urban planning.

It is possible to surmise that people derive benefit from all this interaction, but does this infer *well-being benefits*? There is some evidence to support the idea that people feel better informed and educated, as well as being simply entertained, by visiting heritage attractions – which in turn would seem to fit well with well-being definitions (Britain Thinks/Heritage Lottery Fund, 2015). Moreover, active engagement in heritage projects, such as saving a historic building, has been shown to endow participants with a sense of achievement and resilience (Power and Smyth, 2016). Clearly such benefits might equally be acquired by involvement in projects of other types, but community-based heritage projects that celebrate places and events may be particularly good at generating community cohesion and empowerment. They achieve this by bringing people into contact with others from a variety of backgrounds to focus on a common interest and provide them with a sense of control over decision-making. Heritage-focused projects may also, more broadly, buffer people from what they see as an increasingly precarious world by invoking feelings of permanence and continuity.

Healing

Research examining the healing power of heritage has mostly been carried out in the field of museum studies. This body of work suggests, for example, that visiting museums offers a sense of sanctuary to visitors, stimulating the mind and memory, which in turn has wider well-being benefits (Dodds and Jones, 2014). It is possible that at least some of these benefits might be conferred by historic place more generally, given that historic towns are in one sense museums of historic buildings, places and spaces. However, there is very limited evidence to support this supposition – although one study has suggested that visiting historic towns is positively associated with 'life satisfaction' (as a proxy measure for well-being) (Fujiwara, Cornwall and Dolan, 2014); and, clearly, visiting historic places and living within them are very different experiences.

There have also been a number of projects exploring heritage in healthcare settings and in relation to patient recovery. Such

↑
Figure 6.2
The joy of hugging an old building

studies have demonstrated that heritage objects can enhance the ambience of surroundings and have positive impacts on patients' well-being and physiology (Silverman, 2010). This work emphasises the value of allowing patients to handle objects – to touch them; to provoke stimulation – rather than just look at them (Ander et al., 2013; Paddon et al., 2013). Touch is greatly overlooked in the discipline of urban design, and while of course we may not consciously *handle* historic buildings (perhaps we should?) (Fig.6.2), we do in fact 'touch' historic places all the time, with our hands, feet and indeed buttocks when we sit down, and this interaction deserves more attention and understanding.

Healthcare studies generally involve interaction with a curator, or similar person, to provide 'tailored and easy social interaction' (Ander et al., 2013, p.236). This unlocks potential curiosity towards the objects being studied. In short, both focused physical and verbal interaction would appear to be essential elements in this type of work.

Sense of place/place attachment/identity

A rather more wide-ranging set of evidence is presented around themes of *sense of place*, *place attachment* and *sense of identity*. These inter-related topics present a minefield of terminology and involve competing disciplinary definitions, approaches and discussions of how to measure/value their existence. However, without going into great depth around the attendant complexities, it is perfectly possible to master the main ideas.

In the field of urban design, sense of place – or *genius loci* – tends to focus on local distinctiveness or character. Part of this concerns the materiality of place – local building materials and techniques, different types of building reflecting historical development, wider landscape settings, and so on. However, an equally important aspect is people's engagement with, and lived experience of, that place. In other words, their way of life, the way they speak, the local foodstuffs they consume, local songs, myths and traditions whose origins may be lost in the mists of time, and so on, all play an essential role in defining that place as different to others. As Healey suggests, sense of place is formed by the union of 'physical experiences' and 'imaginative constructions', produced by individual activity and 'socially formed appreciations' (Healey, 2010, p.34). Such processes naturally take time to develop.

In relation to well-being, the proposition is that inhabitants of cities with a strong sense of place will have an equally robust sense of self-rootedness. In other words, a strong sense of place leads to a strong sense of *place attachment* and sense of *identity* (Altman and Low, 1992). This inter-relationship between place, attachment and identity *should* create a solid foundation onto which other elements of well-being can be added. Moreover, research suggests that people form stronger attachments to places that allow them to reach their potential in life (Korpela, 1989). This suggests a virtuous circle between sense of place, attachment, identity and well-being.

Some research has suggested that the existence of local built heritage is an important part of sense of place (Britain Thinks/ Heritage Lottery Fund, 2015), and therefore by the same token is necessary to develop attachment and identity. However, the extent to which the built environment is pre-requisite for sense of identity, and whether, if it is, it can be separately examined, is debatable. As stated in Chapter 1, before becoming an academic I spent several years working in Saltaire, West Yorkshire – a town with a strong and unique sense of place. In talking to, and understanding the mindsets of, residents, I came to realise that, despite the strong historic image of where they lived, residents viewed the town from a very different perspective than myself, in my capacity as a professional charged with the physical conservation of the place itself. In essence, although by their very nature the buildings, and other historic features such as the park, were always there in the stories of life in the village, their uniqueness, their architectural features, even whether they retained certain elements of their historic character, for example, were often of relatively little concern to the residents.

More broadly, however, there is evidence that at the community level historic buildings and structures can imbue communities with a shared sense of history as a source of local pride, even if individuals have not been directly involved with saving them. Their mere presence may engender a sense of ownership and foster a sense of a shared past within the community. This may also contribute to a sense of having an attractive place to live and call home (Britain Thinks/Heritage Lottery Fund, 2015). Research has also suggested that the stability and continuity suggested by visible signs of the past can manifest itself in greater levels of self-esteem and social capital in communities (CURDS/ICCHS, 2009). Moreover, such evidence is particularly strong in areas that have undergone substantial regeneration.

Issues with heritage research
The research work focusing on built heritage is clearly of interest to the broader interests of urban design and well-being. However, it also presents some considerable challenges in terms of extracting what might be applicable to the wider environment and what aspects may have the most positive impacts on well-being. As soon as anything is singled out as special – in the way buildings are listed, for example – people's perception of its value will change, particularly if it then becomes the subject of a project or intervention. However, this does not necessarily tell us very much about how people value the commonplace, anonymous historic buildings that surround us and provide a backdrop to everyday life.

Moreover, when people live and/or work in historic places, they may have little time as they go about their everyday lives to pay much attention to the historic buildings and the streetscape; despite literally being immersed in them, they are generally not the focus of their attention – they are simply there.

—

Reframing the 'benefits' of the past debate
In attempting to reframe the issues around historic places and well-being, one approach is to set aside heritage debates and consider wider narratives about how the past shapes the

present. Here, I suggest the work of historian and geographer David Lowenthal may be helpful. Lowenthal identifies a number of 'benefits' which the past offers us, but also 'burdens', and these are examined later in the chapter (Lowenthal, 1985; Lowenthal, 2015). Since his work is wide-ranging, it does need some interpretation and reworking for application to the built environment, but six themes may be particularly useful. These are: *familiarity*, *reaffirmation*, *identity*, *guidance*, *enrichment* and *escape*. The arguments for these benefits are briefly as follows:

- *Familiarity*   Familiarity renders things recognisable and therefore, at the same time, comprehensible. As a species we have lived in cities for millennia; we understand their form and function. Historic buildings, even unremarkable ones, provide a familiar backdrop against which life is played out, and by this token their presence requires no particular attention – they do not add to the pressures and stresses of life.
- *Reaffirmation*   Reaffirmation, or the validation of what we do today, is supported by links to the activities of our ancestors stretching back into the mists of time – a thread of continuity that links the past, the present and the future. Historic buildings are embodiments of human activity. Even when buildings change their use, we rarely completely erase past activity. Old signs or bits of machinery and redundant technology tend to be left in situ, ratifying our present occupation of them.
- *Identity*   Within this framework, this dimension gives greater emphasis to the notion that part of who we are is who we *were*. Historic buildings and places may contribute to that individual and collective sense of identity by providing evidence of lives past. However, most cities will contain relatively commonplace elements that seem to garner local identity, buildings, place names, and so on, that are unmistakably a part of that place and nowhere else, but are not necessarily earmarked as heritage.

- *Guidance*   The past can be instructive if we allow it to be. Buildings and structures can tell us a great deal, not only about the technology available to previous generations, but the values to which they adhered. For example, the Victorian construction of the railway in central Newcastle – now historic fabric in its own right – involved the destruction of the medieval city walls. This is a physical embodiment of a different relationship between past and present that existed in the 19th century, where confidence in the present outvalued the remnants of the past – a situation to which we are unlikely to return (Fig.6.3).

↑
Figure 6.3
The link between Black Gate (left) and Castle Keep (right).
Newcastle was severed by 19th-century railway infrastructure

- *Enrichment*   Old buildings and places enrich our lives because they are often composed of fabric that would be extremely difficult or impossible to recreate. The ornate railings or the elaborately carved entrance (Fig.6.4) exhibit materials and skills lost in the passage of time. Even if we

↑
Figure 6.4
The joyfully eccentric Emmerson Chambers, Newcastle, c.1903.
Such historic buildings feature materials, ornamentation, and so on,
that would be impossible to reproduce today

can recreate past styles, old buildings develop a patina
(the quality of surfaces brought about by exposure to the
elements and the gradual weathering that ensues) which is
extremely difficult, if not impossible, to fake.

- *Escape*   Finally, old buildings allow us to escape from the
present, even if fleetingly. In our mind's eye we can see past
lives, the things people might have said, the clothes they
might have worn. Books and films (even if highly fanciful
interpretations of history) stimulate our imagination, but
literally walking in the footsteps of the past is equally, if not
more, powerful.

Testing the framework

The Historic Place Benefits Framework is a departure point for exploring people's perceptions and I have used it in my own work, employing photo elicitation research. Here, groups of participants have been shown mixtures of historic and modern city scenes and asked to respond to prompts linked to the Benefits Framework (the research employs the Ombea audience response system).

The work is in the early stages of development and a long way from being publishable, but some issues are emergent. What is clear, for example, is that non-specialist participants find some of the terminology in the Framework too abstract, and rather than using a term such as 'escape', asking a question such as 'how much does this image stimulate your imagination?' (on a sliding scale) elicits clearer and more demarcated results. So, for example, with the prompt 'imagination', people on average rate historic buildings as much more stimulating than newer ones. However, other trends are also discernible. Exceptional historic buildings evoke an exaggerated response, but other elements – for example, the presence of water and other landscape features in the images – stimulate the response even more (Fig.6.5). This suggests that elements other than the building itself are important in triggering people's reactions.

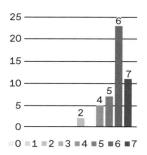

↑
Figure 6.5
Images such as this one of Pulteney Bridge, Bath, reflected in water, score highly in terms of stimulating people's imagination

Note: The vertical axis shows the number of votes; the horizontal axis indicates how strongly the image stimulated the respondents' imagination – 0 being the weakest reaction and 7 being the strongest.

This returns the discussion to how people perceive historic places. Previous research has acknowledged that people may place values on them in ways which may not always be entirely expected. For example, in a US study of people's perceptions of living in a historic district, it was discovered that landscape features such as gates, fountains, trees and gardens evoked a much stronger sense of attachment than the historic buildings themselves (Wells and Baldwin, 2012). On a similar theme, a study of conservation areas in north-east England found that residents ranked the appearance of the buildings in their neighbourhood as only slightly more important than the natural environment; and moreover, social aspects of the area, such as having 'nice neighbours', were actually ranked as more important than the history of the area (Townshend and Pendlebury, 1999). These studies remind us that while historic fabric may often elicit positive emotions and reaction, we must consider environments holistically to understand their well-being impacts.

—

The burdens of the past

While unpacking the benefits of the past around us, we need to consider that the past also carries burdens, albeit ones largely absent, for example, from official heritage and well-being narratives. History is a far from pleasant place. It is littered with violence, tyranny, grinding poverty, premature death, racism, sexism and all kinds of inequity and brutal prejudice against certain groups in society. These issues still impact the lives of people today. Moreover, just as the built environment is an embodiment of the virtues of the past, it also symbolises its very worst aspects; or as J.B. Priestley states, where people have lived a long time, 'the very stones are saturated in evil memories' (Priestley, 1939).

As stated at the beginning of the chapter, the past and 'heritage' are also contested constructs. The term 'dissonant heritage' has been coined to capture that sense of a disputed, debateable nature – drawing on the concept of cognitive dissonance from psychology, which denotes the simultaneous existence of mutually incompatible attitudes (Tunbridge and Ashworth, 1996). In this sense, all heritage belongs to someone, and therefore, logically, there are other groups to whom it does not belong. Moreover, societal attitudes as to what is and what is not acceptable are in constant evolution – thus, one generation's heritage is not necessarily that of the generations who succeed them. All of this should cause us to interrogate what we consider worthy of saving, and how we should save it.

This issue was brought into sharp focus in the wake of the Black Lives Matter campaign of 2020, which was triggered by the death of George Floyd, an African-American man, who was killed by police during an arrest in Minneapolis. In the aftermath, protests were held in cities across the globe – including Bristol, England, a city that benefitted hugely from wealth generated by the historical slave trade. Here, the statue of Edward Colston, a merchant who had made a fortune from the west African slave trade in the late 17th century, was toppled during a demonstration, rolled to the nearby dockside and pushed unceremoniously into the water. The statue was later recovered and, after minimal restoration, has been exhibited in a local museum, along with placards used in the protest. To date the plinth has been left empty (Fig.6.6), although it was briefly occupied by a sculpture of a Black Lives protester that was installed in secret. While there was some condemnation of the way the original Colston statue was removed (particularly by central government), members of the local Black community hailed it as a cathartic act (Bland, 2020).

Statues – and other monuments – are of course particularly poignant because of their often lifelike representation of an individual, which potentially operates as an endorsement of their values. The Colston statue – erected in 1895, over 170 years after Colston's death – had in fact been regarded as controversial for many years, with a number of calls and petitions raised for its removal. His likeness is not alone in this regard.[3] The removal to a museum – where the statue could be presented within a wider context with the aid of explanatory material – does seem like a practical and judicious solution, not

↑
Figure 6.6
The Colston monument, Bristol, after the statue was toppled

least because it allows open debate within the community, while not simply eradicating an uncomfortable element of the past. This was clearly possible in this case because the statue was moveable. However, this is obviously not always the case with historic structures and buildings.

In Liverpool, at about the same time as the toppling of the Colston Statue, street signs at Penny Lane – made famous by a Beatles song of the same name – were also attacked. The reason given for the defacement was that the street was named after James Penny, a Liverpool slave trader. The defacing of the signage itself brought about local protest, not least from nearby residents who consider it part of the local Beatles-related heritage. This caused the Liverpool-based International Slavery Museum to issue a statement that Penny Lane was not named after the individual concerned – or at least suggesting ambiguity as to its origins – even though the connection had been suggested by one of their own exhibits (Dugdale, 2020).

The Penny Lane example is interesting in many ways. First, because it demonstrates that while some aspects of the past are largely undisputed and/or at least well documented, others are much less certain. Street names often carry significant clues about destinations or former activities – York Road or Mill Lane, for example. However, sometimes the apparent connections can be totally spurious: in this case, 'Penny' might not refer to a person's name, but rather to a ubiquitous coin. Perhaps more interestingly is the added layer of Beatles connection; without it, the damage may have gone largely unnoticed and would certainly not have brought it to the attention of the national press.

In some cases it is not just a matter of individual place names, buildings or statues that are the issue. Visiting Dublin in the 1980s, I was naively shocked at how much of the Georgian fabric of the city – away from the pristine Merrion Square on the south side of the city – was in an advanced state of decay. This was not simply the result of economic privation – I am indebted to a very patient member of An Taisce, the National Trust for Ireland, who pointed out that this was an architecture of colonisation and occupation. Two hundred years after the buildings had been constructed by the British, and many decades after their ejection from power, the resentment associated with that period persisted. Interestingly, since this time many of these buildings have been rebuilt and restored, and the city has found a way to reclaim these buildings as its own.

Some cities may have much more of a problem in moving on. Returning to the subject of Bristol, for example, the name 'Colston' was not just associated with a single statue, but with a whole host of institutions, buildings, and so on, which their managers and owners must now consider. Moreover, there will be other equally problematic examples the length and breadth of the country. Where the negative historical association is a matter of record, it will be relatively straightforward to alter the names of streets, buildings, parks, and so on. However, this does run the risk of simply eradicating unpleasant historical events – papering over the cracks, so to speak – rather than addressing them. Ultimately, local communities need to decide for themselves how to deal with the issue. The role of the urban designer is to listen, to understand and to ensure that we react in a meaningful way in our design work.

Conclusions

The past is evident all around us in our towns and cities. That past carries significant benefits, but also imposes burdens on us in the present.

1 *Well-being implications*   The heritage lobby has for some time now highlighted the positive impacts that built heritage has on our well-being. However, while there is some evidence to support these claims, much of the evidence cannot be easily translated into meaningful implications for everyday life.

2 *Local perceptions*   Broader narratives about heritage highlight the benefits that the past may offer us – *familiarity, reaffirmation, identity, guidance, enrichment,* and *escape.* However, built environment professionals need to understand that those who live and work surrounded by historic environments may hold quite different perceptions and value of these places.

3 *Contested places*   The past is also a contested place and one of severe and violent inequity, particularly for certain groups in society. Acknowledging the past and having an open debate about how it is treated is the mark of a mature community. However, it will be a painful and challenging process.

Further reading

Lynch, K. (1972). *What Time Is This Place?* Cambridge, MA: MIT Press.

Pendlebury, J. and J. Brown (2021). *Conserving the Historic Environment.* London: Lund Humphries.

Chapter 7   Towards Health-Promoting – 'Salutogenic' – Cities?

In this chapter we explore inspirational case studies of good practice and briefly reflect on what lessons might be taken from them for broader application, thereby creating cities that are health-promoting, rather than health-suppressing.

Introduction

As illustrated in the previous chapters, there is a significant and growing evidence base that many aspects of contemporary urban living adversely affect human development and constrain people's ability to make healthy lifestyle choices. Significant mistakes have been made in the planning and design of towns and cities in the recent past. The accommodation of the private car has dominated thinking, rather than the needs of human beings. If only the lessons set out in Chapter 1 had been built upon; if all development in the 20th century had met the salutogenic ambitions of garden cities, for example, this volume would not be necessary! However, it is possible to learn from these mistakes and create places that allow people to flourish and lead happier, healthier lives. In short, salutogenic[1] cities are within our grasp.

In this chapter, a series of good practice examples are briefly outlined. These include both projects that have been built and those that are yet to be realised, but demonstrate potential for health and well-being benefits. These are necessarily brief synopses and therefore intended as a starting point for further investigation.

Partnership in action: London's Wild West End Vision

In 2013, the Crown Estate drew up an 'Ecology Masterplan' for its London portfolio, in conjunction with technical advisors Arup. A central element of the plan was to exploit the Crown Estate's substantial property portfolio in the Regent Street area, creating a 'green corridor' connecting Regent's Park to the north with Green Park and St James's Park to the south. While ecology was the departure point for this plan, the key desired outcome was to *improve health and well-being* through access to nature; this remains the key tenet of the scheme.

It became clear that the corridor's potential to generate genetic transfer between sites that were disconnected for hundreds of years before this initiative could be effectively 'supercharged' if adjacent estates undertook complementary projects. This would create a network of opportunities for wildlife between existing and new green spaces across the entire West End district. This led to development of the Wild West End Vision in 2015, requiring the cooperation of, originally, five (currently eight) of the largest property-owning estates in central London. The scheme – now in its sixth year – encourages the installation of green roofs and walls, 'pop-up' landscapes, street trees, planters, and so on.

A baseline survey within the Crown Estate's central London portfolio was carried out in 2014, against which benefits were to be measured, with follow-up surveys in 2016, 2018 and 2021 (ongoing at the time of writing). These surveys track the extent and condition of changes in greenspace provision over time, as well as monitoring the use – human and non-human – of those greenspaces. The work demonstrates that since the baseline survey, the Crown Estate has increased the amount of greenspace in its portfolio by more than 4,000 square metres – representing an astonishing 7,000 per cent increase in an area of some of the most expensive property values in the northern hemisphere. However, there is a recognition that spending on biodiversity and greenspace provision can pay dividends in terms of the property values created and the ease of finding tenants for such property.

The eventual aim is to create a network of spaces – consisting of at least 100 square metres of greenspace – with no more than 100 metres between them across the entire network. This target is described by project ecologist at Arup, Tom Gray, as creating a significant habitat resource, but also 'deliberately ambitious and challenging', in order to keep momentum within the project. Interventions are required to meet two or more aspects of a 'value matrix' of functions – including biodiversity, climate mitigation, microclimate improvement, well-being and social purposes (Wild West End, 2021).

The scheme was expanded in June 2020 when eight Business Improvement Districts (BIDs) and partnerships joined the Wild West End project, further extending its reach across the capital. The commercial partners work in a strategic alliance with the Greater London Authority and the London Wildlife Trust charity, with technical support for the project supplied by Arup.

One (temporary) installation was that of an award-winning garden originally showcased at the Chelsea Flower Show in 2018, designed by Kate Gould. The garden was installed for 18

↑
Figure 7.1
Wild West End Garden installation, Old Quebec Street

months at Old Quebec Street, located at the Marble Arch end of Oxford Street (Fig 7.1) – some elements, such as the planters, remain in place. Monitoring carried out by Arup established that the number of people walking through the street per day at this location increased by 47 per cent, and 'dwell time' in the street increased by 29 per cent. Self-reported well-being in the street rose by 64 per cent; and while a multi-item scale of well-being returned a much more modest increase of 2 per cent, comparing pre- and post-installation, this is still significant (Arup, 2019). Monitoring of another greening project, which has transformed Glasshouse Street/Air Street in neighbouring Soho from a dingy backwater to a pedestrian-friendly thoroughfare, has delivered similar results.

Takeaway messages – multi-disciplinarity and partnership working

The scheme demonstrates that even when rival commercial organisations work in partnership, mutually beneficial outcomes can be created – not only economic, but social and ecological. The project also demonstrates the holistic benefits of bringing multi-disciplinary teams together in the development process.

Though challenging, similar projects may work outside the capital, particularly where there are large land-holders who are able to carry out interventions on their estate – these would include, for example, educational institutions, hospitals and infrastructure providers.

—

Cost-effective active travel: Connswater Community Greenway, Belfast

The concept for the Connswater Community Greenway was first put forward c.2005–6 by the Eastside Partnership Belfast (EPB), a broad-based social partnership with community, statutory, political and business members. Subsequently, National Lottery funding was secured to create a 9-kilometre linear park through the city following the course of the Connswater, Knock and Loop

↑
Figure 7.2
Sam Thompson Bridge, Belfast – part of the Connswater route

Rivers, connecting green spaces and remediating flood risk (Fig.7.2). The scheme aimed to benefit the 40,000 people living in the administrative wards adjacent to the river, creating a valuable local amenity and providing opportunities for improving health and well-being.

The scheme has been used as a natural experiment in the Physical Activity and Rejuvenation of Connswater (PARC) study. This research, carried out by Queen's University in Belfast, commenced in 2010 before the construction of the Greenway. Early on in the scheme, modelling of potential health outcomes was carried out based on local residents' physical activity patterns, which indicated that 35 per cent of men and 53 per cent of women were not meeting minimum guidelines for physical activity prior to the development of the project. One study that explored objective and subjective motivations for walking suggested that the scheme model would increase inactive individuals' moderate physical activity by an estimated 39 minutes per week, representing a 35 per cent increase from existing levels (Longo et al., 2015).

In other research, it was estimated that changing a resident from being inactive to active would reduce the likelihood of a range of diseases over a 40-year period, resulting in an additional 46 years not impacted by disability gained for the catchment population. Importantly, the cost-effectiveness analysis indicated that the project was good value for money, with all outcomes modelled coming in at below £20,000–£30,000 per quality adjusted life-year (Dallat et al., 2014). More recent evidence from the PARC study showed a twofold increase in use of the greenway between 2010 and 2017. The study has been cautious in its conclusions regarding health/well-being benefits; however, the current estimate is that if just 2 per cent of local residents become more active, then the scheme will in essence pay for itself (Simpson, 2019).

Takeaway messages from Connswater

The scheme shows what private/public/community partnerships can achieve. Since the COVID-19 crisis there has been considerable backlash against some active travel schemes instigated by local authorities during the pandemic (see, for example, McIntyre, 2020). The popularity of Connswater demonstrates the need for community 'buy-in'. Moreover, and while still not proven, early indications are that such schemes can be highly cost-effective in terms of reducing the burden of chronic disease in communities.

—

A whole systems approach: Bicester NHS Healthy New Town

NHS Healthy New Towns were launched in 2015 with 10 demonstrator projects, including Bicester, Oxfordshire. Healthy New Towns seek to build partnerships, governance structures, delivery plans and interventions to drive forward healthy place-making strategies. In Bicester, this has been set around three work streams – built environment, community activation, and new models of care (NHS, 2019). Bicester also set out two key targets:

- To increase the number of physically active children and adults and those at a healthy weight.
- To reduce the number of people feeling socially isolated/ lonely, and improve mental well-being.

It is worth noting that prior to Healthy New Town status, Bicester had already been awarded Garden Town status in 2014 – as a key growth area to receive government funding. Furthermore, Bicester Eco Village – a unique development built in line with the Eco Towns Planning Policy Statement (PPS) before it was scrapped in 2015 – was already in development. While the Healthy New Town status was undoubtedly linked to the success of the Eco Town project, it did mean that certain aspects of the built environment workstream had to be effectively 'retrofitted'. Positively, research funded by the Natural Environment Research Council (NERC) and carried out in 2016–18 by the University of Oxford Environmental Change Institute provided strong evidence that Bicester's network of greenspaces were already providing a range of health and well-being benefits (Smith et al., n.d.).

In terms of the built environment, a series of initiatives have been delivered including three 5K health routes, cycling and walking initiatives, and two green gyms. Community action initiatives include work with schools, businesses and third sector organisations to promote physical activity and healthier eating, and improve mental health. For new models of care, joined-up planning between the Clinical Commissioning Group, primary care practices, local planners and councillors to develop primary care facilities that are future-proofed has been instigated; new social prescribing has been introduced; as have care pathways, for example, for patients with diabetes, among a raft of other delivery innovations.

The programme was originally conceptualised as a multi-component intervention to improve local health, but has evolved into a 'systems-wide' approach to promoting health within the community (Rowe, 2019). Rosie Rowe, Programme Director for Healthy Bicester, describes healthy place-making as a 'systems connector', joining up all the relevant actors. Currently, the whole system is being mapped and will be available in full and summary versions in due course.

The full impact of Bicester's Healthy New Town programme will not be known for many years; however, it is of importance that evaluation has been embedded into the programme from the outset and is designed to capture a wide range of process and output metrics. Early evaluation is positive, for example, demonstrating increases in physical activity among the local population – one measure of this is that pedestrian use of the health routes has increased by 27 per cent (Rowe, 2019). Scaling up the approach to include other areas within Cherwell District Council has also already begun, including the planned expansion of Kidlington village. This will incorporate learning from the experiences at Bicester and ensure that only evidenced-based interventions are adopted.

Takeaway messages from Bicester Healthy New Town
Changing systems takes time and resources, especially if many actors in the system have to accustom themselves to new ways of working. Building and sustaining relationships is therefore key.

—

Increasing well-being through temporary intervention: Stalled Spaces Project, Glasgow (relaunched 2021)
In many larger, post-industrial cities there are pockets of under-used, vacant and/or derelict land. One approach to this is to allow temporary – sometimes referred to as 'meanwhile' – uses to occupy these spaces. The Glasgow 'Stalled Spaces' programme was introduced by the City Council in 2010, partly as a positive reaction to the economic crash of 2008, at which point 60 per cent of Glasgow's population was living within 500 metres of a vacant/derelict site. The scheme built on a pre-existing programme to improve 'backcourt' areas in poorer communities. This had highlighted the negative health/well-being impacts of under-used/derelict sites, and/or sites awaiting development.

The aim of the Stalled Spaces scheme was to support community groups and local organisations in developing their own *temporary* projects on these sites. A range of projects were proposed as acceptable, from pop-up gardens, gyms and play spaces to art installations (Glasgow City Council, 2021). However, a key aim was to improve community health and well-being, for example, by encouraging interaction with greenspace, promoting physical activity and improving social interaction. Communities were offered a grant of up to £4,500, although this was subject to certain protocols – for example, being a registered charity and having a governance structure.

Over the first 10 years approximately £500,000 of funds were allocated to groups and organisations, and in turn this helped to deliver over 125 projects, representing interventions on over 25 hectares of vacant land. The principles of Stalled Spaces have also been taken to other Scottish authorities through the work of Architecture and Design Scotland (2020), though Glasgow remains at the forefront of development. Early research on the impact of the programme – carried out by the Glasgow Centre for Population Health – was encouraging, stating that 90 per cent of participants in the projects surveyed felt that their participation had a 'quite positive' or a 'very positive' influence on their well-being, and 75 per cent of people reported that they had become more connected and active within their community (Yates, 2015).

In parallel to Stalled Spaces, the City Council has also been a lead authority in 'Connecting Nature', a pan-global project investing in large-scale implementation of nature-based projects in urban settings. This, in turn, has developed an Impact Assessment Guidebook for nature-based solutions, which sets out a framework for the robust monitoring and evaluation of such projects (Connecting Nature, n.d.). A key element of the framework is the division of projects into three stages – planning, delivery and stewardship – and the Connecting Nature project was tasked with a review of Stalled Spaces using the framework; this was carried out in 2019/20.

The review revealed that, although much good work had been achieved, there were also significant problems. For example, protocols put in place – as outlined above and based on other Council small grant schemes – effectively acted as a barrier to getting involved for many communities. Some schemes had been effectively 'one-day events', and some had actually left the sites in a worse condition than they were before intervention, leaving communities disappointed and disillusioned. Gillian Dick, the current programme lead, explained: 'when communities were given the grant, they were simply left to get on with it, we didn't ask them what continued support they needed . . . we didn't investigate what they needed to become resilient and to grow'. As a result some schemes had requested repeat grants in order to survive, but had not become self-sustaining.

The advent of the coronavirus pandemic in 2020 effectively stalled progress, but the project team used this time wisely to take stock and address shortcomings. The result was that, based on the review findings, the project was relaunched in Spring 2021. Three larger, more strategic projects were funded, working through third sector organisations running in-depth investigations into the needs and aspirations of the communities where they were embedded; these were Drumchapel, Pollok and South Central. These projects were ongoing at the time of writing, but a key aim was to effectively 'map out' community activities and look at opportunities to 'bundle' projects together to apply for larger funding grants. The authority has already launched a Connecting Nature Dashboard[2] which will incorporate data from the next generation of Stalled Spaces projects and allow direct correlation between pertinent data sets and evidence benefits derived from future schemes.

Takeaway messages from Stalled Spaces

- Early successes and positive outcomes of the Stalled Spaces programme showed in principle that the scheme is viable and can have positive impacts on community health and well-being. However, during the first phase of the scheme, data collection was inconsistent, resulting in a lost opportunity for project evaluation.

- Proper and robust monitoring and evaluation are key to building on success – the new Connecting Nature Dashboard is a good example of how to visualise this.

Community aspirations for healthy homes in the future: Oakfield, Swindon, and Selby Urban Village, Haringey

Oakfield, Swindon
Oakfield aims to be a new model of housing delivery, one that the developer, the building society Nationwide, has labelled, 'not for profit, socially responsible housing' (Nationwide Building Society, 2020); a summary of the approach is set out in Figure 7.3. Working with development partner Igloo, the scheme will deliver 239 homes on a brownfield site – a former college campus – approximately three kilometres due east of Swindon railway station. It is intended that 30 per cent of the properties will be set at an affordable rent, or for purchase through shared ownership. The scheme incorporates a substantial landscaped central green corridor –a network of shared and private greenspaces as well as paths and cycleways which integrate the development into surrounding neighbourhoods.

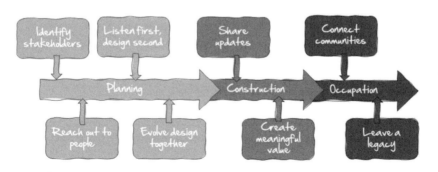

↑
Figure 7.3
Nationwide's development approach at Oakfield

There was an extensive public engagement and collaborative design development process with surrounding local communities in the 18 months prior to the submission of a planning application. This not only involved the usual type of exhibition/engagement events, but significantly the embedding of a community organiser (Keith Brown) within the surrounding neighbourhoods. Keith collected vast quantities of invaluable information from those communities, directly speaking to residents in their homes and at places where people naturally gathered. This enabled a much broader range of people – crucially including those who felt disenfranchised from mainstream community participation routes – to be included. Katherine Quigley, Social Investment Manager with Nationwide Building Society, states that a 'number' of key design decisions were taken based on community input. Several of these had a direct health/well-being impact, including:

- Intergenerational mixing, rather than separating out older persons' accommodation – for example, having different age groups living within the same apartment block.
- Offering a choice between larger private gardens, or smaller private gardens with access to a shared garden beyond – allowing residents space to mix.
- Making sure that all public spaces are overlooked to ensure their use.
- The integration of multiple places with seating, so as to encourage serendipitous encounters.
- Paired front doors – again to encourage communication between neighbours.
- A community hub – available to both new residents and those from the surrounding area.
- Detailed design interventions – for example, including electric cycle charging points in all garden sheds.
- Hierarchical location of shared (pedestrian/traffic) spaces – (following consultation with visual impairment groups) – so that they are restricted to areas where traffic will be naturally slow, and people will feel confident to use them.

↑
Figure 7.4
Artist's impression of Oakfield development, foregrounding open space for
children's play and physical activity, social interaction and relaxation

- Local schoolchildren were also consulted during the design
  process, choosing natural feeling play equipment and
  spaces, and an outdoor gym.

Overall there was a desire for maximum greenspace inclusion
from multiple perspectives (Fig.7.4).

At the time of writing this was in the initial stages of
development, working with residents on a community charter and
developing the principles of shared gardens. A baseline survey
– including some health/well-being self-reporting – has been
carried out, with follow-up annual monitoring planned; the first
residents should be on site by Spring 2022. The data gathered
by this will be invaluable for future research. Nationwide is also
currently developing a blueprint for similar delivery, to share with
like-minded developers.

Takeaway message from Oakfield
Involving the local community thoroughly at an early stage can
improve the end product (and ease the passage through planning:
not a single objection to the scheme was received, reducing
costs at the planning stage of the project). However, this type

of community engagement is complex, and reaching out needs commitment by the developer that goes well beyond usual participation practices.

Selby Urban Village, Haringey

At the time of writing, Selby Urban Village is in the pre-planning stage. At the heart of the 1.58-hectare site lies Selby Centre, a former 1970s school which is run by Selby Trust. It was established in 1992 and provides an umbrella organisation for around 35 third sector groups and businesses that are housed in the former classrooms. Working with Selby Centre has been central to the thinking behind a new vision of the area by Karakusevic Carson Architects and for client Haringey Council as landowners; and community involvement has been extensive (Fig.7.5).

The centre will remain at the heart of the community, with playing fields to the north reconfigured for a range of sports and recreation uses for healthy exercise; additionally, spaces for exercise and socialisation will be designed in throughout the necessarily dense surrounding housing. The aim is to allow for

←
Figure 7.5
Co-design workshop –
Selby Urban Village

serendipitous encounters and to foster a neighbourhood-wide sense of community through the overlapping and interlocking of everyday life and juxtaposition of widely different activities next to each other (for more information, see Karakusevic, Althorpe and Batchelor, 2021). The realisation of the plan will, however, require thoughtful negotiation and a strong degree of municipal cooperation since, while Haringey Council are the landowners, part of the site lies within the administrative boundaries of neighbouring Enfield.

Takeaway message from Selby Urban Village
It is possible to think beyond the traditional model of a community centre, set within an otherwise residential development, to a neighbourhood where community participation is implicated in the everyday lives of residents.

—

Mayfield, Manchester: a city centre fit for the future
Manchester's Mayfield is a large, complex, mixed-used regeneration project, centred on 24 acres of former railway infrastructure, south-east of Manchester Piccadilly station. The development will create approximately 150,000 square metres of offices (equating to 10,000 job spaces), 1,500 new homes and a range of new shops, bars, restaurants and other services. The details of these are still in the design stage; however, the vision is for a socially and economically mixed community, with a wide range of accommodation, from single-person apartments to – and unusually in central locations in the UK – family housing.

The project will reuse pre-existing railway heritage – parts of the former Mayfield station – where appropriate. At the heart of the site, a 2.8-hectare public park – the largest to be built in the city since the 19th century – is under construction at the time of writing. When complete, this will include: space for physical activity (sports as well as informal play); floodable meadows and biodiverse ecological areas; and quieter spaces for escape and contemplation. Sheltered structures and areas will ensure use in all weathers and seasons (Fig.7.6).

↑
Figure 7.6
The park at the heart of the proposed Mayfield development, Manchester

Martyn Evans, Creative Director at U+I plc, the development company behind the scheme, states that the approach aims to create places that replicate those qualities that occur naturally when towns and villages develop organically – and unplanned – over long periods of time. Moreover, health and well-being are central to the planning and design for the project. He states: 'the way we operate is the way we think everyone should approach property development: it's not a proprietary product . . . it's for the good of communities and people's well-being . . .' However, he further states that as far as he is concerned, this is also the key to commercial success, because places that respond to individual and community needs are more likely to flourish, and this will return a better profit to investors and shareholders.

The Mayfield development is a partnership between public land and private ownership which the developers see as key to unlocking current development potential, and a significant element of this has been the development of the public park which has been kick-started by a grant of £23 million from central government. However, the returns from the project to the public purse are estimated to be substantial in terms of jobs created and, therefore, tax paid. Evans states that a key element of the success of unlocking public money was the quality of the economic case put forward by Greater Manchester Combined Authority (GMCA) in their own investment strategy.

The value of the property surrounding the park is estimated at £1.4 billion, although in the current climate no property investor would be willing to finance its construction, entailing that the park had to be built first. The park will therefore be key to attracting residents and allowing a community to flourish – however, it is also key to letting the surrounding office space. Evans states that COVID-19 has accelerated changes in office environments. In many sectors, human resources departments have become as important as financial ones in decision-making, and creating workspaces that are attractive and conducive to good health and well-being are important in attracting the right staff.

Takeaway message from Mayfield, Manchester
Partnership as a key to success is emphasised again, as is the fact that the development involves a team from a wide range of disciplinary backgrounds – from health and well-being consultants, to artists, to engineers.

Here, as in other arenas, COVID-19 has accelerated trends. The user-friendly, 'ping-pong tables for breaks'-type office as associated with trendy tech companies in the last decade has spread – office providers in competitive industries need to cater for staff well-being.

—

Concluding thoughts
Twenty years ago, when I made something of a leap of faith from mainstream conservation/built environment research to focus on health and well-being, there was a scarcity of academic publications in the field, and practical built examples of schemes aiming to design in greater well-being were non-existent. Many built environment colleagues openly expressed the opinion that

I was on the wrong track. Practitioners suggested that human health was something that was 'intuitively' built into everyday practice, while academic colleagues asserted that health and well-being was merely a sub-category of concerns covered by the much broader sustainability agenda. Fortunately, this is no longer the case. Perspectives on health and well-being have shifted significantly, and if there were any lingering doubts that we need to focus more acutely on health in the field of urban design and planning, then, tragically, in the wake of COVID-19, these will have largely fallen away.

I would like, therefore, to end this volume on an entirely optimistic note, but in all honesty I cannot. The coronavirus pandemic is a wake-up call: we must build our towns and cities differently in the future – the examples contained in this chapter are encouraging, but they are still the exception and not the rule. Despite the UK government's promises to 'build back better', in terms of the built environment, there is no clear lead. The recently published *National Model Design Code* (MHCLG, 2021) – much vaunted by the government as the way to improve the quality of places – barely mentions health. More worryingly, a raft of changes have been proposed that will considerably weaken an already over-stretched and under-resourced planning system. The impact of this would be *more* poor-quality developments that do not support health and well-being, against which developers trying to do the right thing will have to compete. I hope I am proved wrong. Salutogenic cities are within our grasp, and there is plenty of evidence that communities aspire to live in them. It is time for all of us with an interest in the built environment – whatever our background, or discipline – to meet the challenge!

Notes

1 Lessons from History: Special Places to Everyday Spaces

1. Note that this is a clear departure from prevailing views of the day.

2. A movement against the consumption of alcohol which flourished in the 19th and early 20th centuries.

3. As a Quaker, Cadbury was opposed to the consumption of alcohol.

4. Classical planning inspired by the 19th-century École des Beaux-Arts, Paris.

2 Definitions and Measures

1. The set of causes, or manner of causation, of a disease.

2. In other words, a range of flora, waterbodies and so on.

3 Active Lives, Active Travel

1. Natural experiments are interventions not designed for research, but which nevertheless provide valuable research opportunities. Sustrans' Connect2 project has been studied by the iConnect research consortium of universities, see https://www.southampton.ac.uk/engineering/research/projects/iconnect.page

4 The Need for Healthy Homes and High Streets

1. While the term 'home' is used to imply place of residence for individuals or families, the term 'housing' is used by the government in relation to the measurement of circumstances and conditions of homes.

2. The Decent Homes Standard guidance was published in 2006 and is undergoing review at the time of writing (2021). It sets minimum standards for the age of bathrooms and kitchens, as well as aspects such as noise insulation and thermal performance.

3. The companies that dominate the UK housing market, accounting for around 60 per cent of all newly built homes for private sale.

4. Permitted development means that, subject to certain criteria being met, the development can go ahead without going through the usual process of applying for planning permission.

5. A movement begun in the US in the 1990s concerned with a return to traditional city design. See the Congress for New Urbanism (CNU), https://www.cnu.org/

6 The Benefits and Burdens of the Past: Heritage, Place and Well-being

1. Ironically, with the passage of time, this book has become much less well-known than some of his other writing, although it is strongly recommended reading.

2. This may be seen in a context of wider narratives that seek to promote the socially progressive potential of the heritage movement.

3. It is not alone – a similar campaign to remove a statue of the imperialist Cecil Rhodes at Oxford University was successfully mounted, although this time with official sanction from the governing body of Oriel College, where it was located. Many authorities have begun reviews of statues under their jurisdiction.

7 Towards Health-Promoting – 'Salutogenic' – Cities?

1. 'Salutogenic' – or focused on health promotion and factors that support human health and well-being – is a term first coined by medical sociologist Aaron Antonovsky, who outlined how humans can turn around the most deeply negative of life experiences.

2. For Connecting Nature Dashboard, see https://connectingnature.eu/sites/default/files/images/inline/Impact%20brochure%20-%20Draft%201.pdf

References

Abbott, J., P. Davies, P. Simkins, C. Morgan, D. Levin and P. Robinson (n.d.). *Creating Water Sensitive Places – Scoping the Potential for Water Sensitive Urban Design in the UK.* London: CIRIA.

Aldred, R., J. Croft and A. Goodman (2019). 'Impacts of an Active Travel Intervention with a Cycling Focus in a Suburban Context: One-year Findings from an Evaluation of London's In-progress Mini-Hollands Programme', *Transportation Research Part A: Policy and Practice* 123, pp 147–69.

Alt, P.L. (2017). 'Sacred Space and the Healing Journey', *Annals of Palliative Medicine* 6(3), pp 284–96.

Altman, I. and S.M. Low (eds) (1992). *Place Attachment.* New York: Plenum Press.

Ander, E., L. Thomson, G. Noble, A. Lanceley, U. Menon and H. Chatterjee (2013). 'Heritage, Health and Well-being: Assessing the Impact of a Heritage Focused Intervention on Health and Well-Being', *International Journal of Heritage Studies* 19(3), pp 229–37.

Annerstedt, M., P. Jönsson, M. Wallergård, G. Johansson, B. Karlson, P. Grahn, et al. (2013). 'Inducing Physiological Stress Recovery with Sounds of Nature in a Virtual Reality Forest – Results from a Pilot Study', *Physiology and Behavior* 118, pp 240–50.

Appleton, J. (1975). *The Experience of Landscape.* Chichester: Wiley & Sons.

Architecture and Design Scotland (2020). 'Stalled Spaces Scotland', https://www.ads.org.uk/stalled-spaces-scotland/

ARUP (2019). 'Wild West End Garden: Monitoring Old Quebec Street'. London: ARUP.

Aspinall, P., P. Mavros, R. Coyne and J. Roe (2015). 'The Urban Brain: Analysing Outdoor Physical Activity with Mobile EEG', *British Journal of Sports Medicine* 49(4), pp 272–6.

Bancroft, C., S. Joshi, A. Rundle, M. Hutson, C. Chong, C.C. Weiss, et al. (2015). 'Association of Proximity and Density of Parks and Objectively Measured Physical Activity in the United States: A Systematic Review', *Social Science & Medicine* 138, pp 22–30.

Barton, H. and M. Grant (2006). 'A Health Map for the Local Human Habitat', *Journal of the Royal Society for the Promotion of Health* 126(6), pp 252–3.

Barton, H., M. Grant and R. Guise (2010). *Shaping Neighbourhoods for Local Health and Global Sustainability.* Abingdon: Routledge.

Barton, H., M. Horswell and P. Millar (2012). 'Neighbourhood Accessibility and Active Travel', *Planning Practice and Research* 27, pp 177–201.

Beevers, R. (1988). *The Garden City Utopia: A Critical Biography of Ebenezer Howard.* Basingstoke: Macmillan.

Berman, M.G., J. Jonides and S. Kaplan (2008). 'The Cognitive Benefits of Interacting with Nature', *Psychological Science* 19(12), pp 1207–12.

Bland, A. (2020). 'The Fall of Colston's Statue – It Didn't Take Long, About Four Tugs of the Rope', *The Guardian*, 9 June.

Britain Thinks/Heritage Lottery Fund (2015). '20 Years in 12 Places', https://www.heritagefund.org.uk/sites/default/files/media/attachments/final_4-hlf_20-years_12-places-access_0.pdf

Burdette, A.M., T.D. Hill and L. Hale (2011). 'Household Disrepair and the Mental Health of Low-Income Urban Women', *Journal of Urban Health* 88(1), pp 142–53.

Burgoine, T., N.G. Forouhi, S.J. Griffin, S. Brage, N.J.

References

Wareham and P. Monsivais (2016). 'Does Neighborhood Fast-Food Outlet Exposure Amplify Inequalities in Diet and Obesity? A Cross-sectional Study', *The American Journal of Clinical Nutrition* 6(103), pp 1540–47.

Carmichael, L., T.G. Townshend, T.B. Fischer, K. Lock, C. Petrokofsky, A. Sheppard, D. Sweeting and F. Ogilvie (2019). 'Urban Planning as an Enabler of Urban Health: Challenges and Good Practice in England Following the 2012 Planning and Public Health Reforms', *Land Use Policy* 84, pp 154–62.

Cerevero, R. and K. Kochelman (1997). 'Travel Demand and the 3Ds: Density, Diversity and Design', *Transport Research* 2(3), pp 199–219.

Chadwick, E. ([1842]2012). *Report on the Sanitary Conditions of the Labouring Population of Great Britain*. London: Forgotten Books.

Chance, H. (2012). 'Mobilising the Modern Industrial Landscape for Sports and Leisure in the Early Twentieth Century', *The International Journal of the History of Sport* 29(11), pp 1600–1625.

Cherry, G. (1996). 'Bournville, England, 1895–1995', *Journal of Urban History* 22(4), pp 493–508.

Clark, C., C. Crumpler and H. Notley (2020). 'Evidence for Environmental Noise Effects on Health for the United Kingdom Policy Context: A Systematic Review of the Effects of Environmental Noise on Mental Health, Wellbeing, Quality of Life, Cancer, Dementia, Birth, Reproductive Outcomes, and Cognition', *International Journal of Environmental Research and Public Health* 17(2), p.34.

Congress internationaux d'architecture moderne (CIAM). The Athens Charter, 1933. Trans. J. Tyrwhitt. Paris, France. The Library of the Graduate School of Design, Harvard University, 1946.

Conisbee, M., P. Kjell, J. Oram, J. Bridges-Palmer, A. Simms and J. Taylor (2005). *Clone Town Britain: The Loss of Local Identity on the Nation's High Streets*. London: New Economics Foundation.

Connecting Nature (n.d.). Connecting Nature Impact Assessment Guidebook, https://connectingnature.eu/sites/default/files/images/inline/Impact%20brochure%20-%20Draft%201.pdf

Cooper Marcus, C. and N.A. Sachs (2014). *Therapeutic Landscapes*. Hillsdale, NJ: John Wiley & Sons.

Cunliffe, B. (1984). *Roman Bath Discovered*. London: Routledge and Kegan Paul.

CURDS/ICCHS (2009). *Sense of Place and Social Capital and the Historic Built Environment: Report of Research for English Heritage*, https://historicengland.org.uk/content/heritage-counts/pub/sense_of_place_web-pdf/

Dahlgren, G. and M. Whitehead (1991). *Policies and Strategies to Promote Social Equity in Health*. Stockholm: Institute for Futures Studies.

Dallat, M.A.T., I. Soerjomataram, R.F. Hunter, M.A. Tully, K.J. Cairns and F. Kee (2014). 'Urban Greenways Have the Potential to Increase Physical Activity Levels Cost-Effectively', *European Journal of Public Health* 24, pp 190–95.

Darley, G. (2007). *Villages of Vision: A Study of Strange Utopias*. Nottingham: Five Leaves.

DCLG (2006). *A Decent Home: Definition and Guidance for Implementation*. London: DCLG.

Deci, E.L. and R.M. Ryan (2008). 'Hedonia, Eudaimonia, and Well-being: An Introduction', *Journal of Happiness Studies* 9, pp 1–11.

Department for Transport (2018). 'Statistical Release: Reported Road Casualties in Great Britain, Quarterly Provisional Estimates Year Ending June 2018', https://assets.publishing.service.gov.uk/government/uploads/system/uploads/attachment_data/file/754685/quarterly-estimates-april-to-june-2018.pdf.

Diener, E. (1984). 'Subjective Well-being', *Psychological Bulletin* 95, pp 542–75.

Ding, D., K. Gebel, P. Phongsavan, A.E. Bauman and D. Merom (2014). 'Driving: A Road to Unhealthy Lifestyles and Poor Health Outcomes', *Plos One* 9(6), pp 1–5.

Dodds, J. and C. Jones (2014). *Mind, Body, Spirit: How Museums Impact Health and Well-Being*. Leicester: Research Centre for Museums and Galleries (RCMG), University of Leicester.

Dugdale, J. (2020). 'Reflecting, Reviewing, Responding', National Museums Liverpool, https://www.liverpool museums.org.uk/stories/reflecting-reviewing-and-responding

Duncan, M. (2011). 'The Cost Saving Potential of Car-sharing in a US Context', *Transportation* 38(2), pp 363–82.

Ellaway, A., M. Benzeval, M. Green, A. Leyland and S. Macintyre (2012). 'Getting Sicker Quicker: Does Living in a More Deprived Neighbourhood Mean Your Health Deteriorates Faster?', *Health & Place* 18(2), pp 132–7.

Ellis, R.B, S.P. Greaves and D.A. Hensher (2013). 'Five Years of London's Low Emission Zone: Effects on Vehicle Fleet Composition and Air Quality', *Transport Research Part D* 23, pp 25–33.

Engels, F. ([1845]1987). *The Condition of the Working Class in England*. Harmondsworth: Penguin Classics.

Essex Tuck-In (2021). Essex Tuck-In, https://www. livewellcampaign.co.uk/pioneering-healthy-eating-initiative-short listed-for-national-award/

Fainie, G.A., D.J.R. Wilby and L.E. Saunders (2016). 'Active Travel in London: The Role of Travel: Survey Data in Describing Population Physical Activity', *Journal of Transport and Health* 3(2), pp 161–72.

Fujiwara, D., T. Cornwall and P. Dolan (2014). *Heritage and Wellbeing*. London: Historic England.

Gateshead Council (2015). *Hot Food Takeaway Supplementary Planning Document*. Gateshead: Gateshead Council.

Geddes, P. (1949). *Cities in Evolution*. London: Williams and Norgate.

Gerodetti, N. and S. Foster (2016). '"Growing Foods from Home": Food Production, Migrants and the Changing Cultural Landscapes of Gardens and Allotments', *Landscape Research* 41(7), pp 808–19.

Gibson, J.J. (1979). *The Ecological Approach to Visual Perception*. Hillsdale, NJ: Lawrence Erlbaum Associates.

Gilbert, E. and S. Galea (2014). 'Urban Neighborhoods and Mental Health across the Life Course'. In: R. Cooper, E. Burton and C. Cooper (eds), *Wellbeing: A Complete Reference Guide, Volume II*. Chichester: Wiley-Blackwell.

Glasgow City Council (2021). 'Stalled Spaces Glasgow', https://www.glasgow.gov.uk/stalledspaces

Goodman, A., J. Panter, S.J. Sharp and D. Ogilvie (2013). 'Effectiveness and Equity Impacts of Town-Wide Cycling Initiatives in England: A Longitudinal, Controlled, Natural Experimental Study', *Social Science & Medicine* 97, pp 228–37.

Goodman, A., S. Sahlqvist and D. Ogilvie, iConnect Consortium (2014). 'New Walking and Cycling Routes and Increased Physical Activity: One- and 2-Year Findings From the UK iConnect Study', *American Journal of Public Health* 104(9), pp e38–e46.

Gov.UK (2016). 'Green Infrastructure', *Natural Environment*, https://www.gov.uk/guidance/natural-environment #green-infrastructure, updated 2019.

Gov.UK (2019). *Clean Air Strategy 2019*, 14 January, https://www.gov.uk/government/publications/clean-air-strategy-2019

Gov.UK (2021). *Fuel Poverty Statistics*, https://www.gov.uk/government/collections/fuel-poverty-statistics

Grayling, T., K. Hallam, D. Graham, R. Anderson and S. Glaister (2002). *Streets Ahead: Safe and Liveable Streets for Children*. London: IPPR.

Hall, P. (2014). *Cities of Tomorrow: An Intellectual History of Urban Planning* and Design Since 1880. Chichester: Wiley-Blackwell.

Halonen, J.I., M. Kivimaki, J. Penti, S. Stenholm, I. Kawachi, S.V. Subramanian, et al. (2014). 'Green and Blue Areas for Predictors of Overweight and Obesity in an 8-Year Follow-Up Study', Obesity 22, pp 1910–17.

Halpern, D. (1995). Mental Health and the Built Environment: More than Bricks and Mortar. London: Taylor and Francis.

Hancock, T. and L.J. Duhl (1988). Promoting Health in the Urban Context. Copenhagen: FADL.

Haringey Council (2011). Scrutiny Review of the Clustering of Betting Shops in Haringey. London: London Borough of Haringey.

Harman, H. (2011). 'The Problem of Betting Shops Blighting High Streets and Communities in Low-Income Areas', https://fairergambling.org/wp-content/uploads/2012/12/Annex-1-Harriet-Harman-Constituency-Report.pdf

Hartig, T., G.W. Evans, L.D. Jamner, D.S. Davis and T. Garling (2003). 'Tracking Restoration in Natural and Urban Field Settings', Journal of Environmental Psychology 23(2), pp 109–23.

Hathaway, E. and S. Sharples (2012). 'The Interaction of Urban Form and Rivers in the Mitigation of the Heat Island Effect: A UK Case Study', Building and Environment 58, pp 14–22.

Haynes, E.N., A. Chen, P. Ryan, P. Succop, J. Wright and K.N. Dietrich (2011). 'Exposure to Airborne Metals and Particulate Matter and Risk for Youth Adjudicated for Criminal Activity', Environmental Research 111(8), pp 1243–8.

Healey, P. (2010). Making Better Places. Basingstoke: Palgrave Macmillan.

Helliwell, J., R. Layard and J. Sachs (2019). World Happiness Report. New York: Sustainable Development Solutions Network.

Henschel, S., G. Chan and World Health Organization Regional Office for Europe (2013). 'Health Risks of Air Pollution in Europe — HRAPIE Project: New Emerging Risks to Health from Air Pollution – Results from the Survey of Experts'. Copenhagen: WHO Regional Office for Europe, https://apps.who.int/iris/handle/10665/108632

Hollinghurst, J., R. Fry, A. Akbari, A. Watkins, N. Williams, S. Hillcoat-Nallétamby, et al. (2020). 'Do Home Modifications Reduce Care Home Admissions for Older People? A Matched Control Evaluation of the Care & Repair Cymru Service in Wales', Age and Ageing 49(6), pp 1056–61.

Howard, E. (2009). Garden Cities of To-Morrow (Illustrated Edition). London: Dodo Press.

Hubbard, E. and M. Shippobottom (2005). A Guide to Port Sunlight Village. Liverpool: Liverpool University Press.

Jackson, R. (1990). 'Waters and Spas in the Classical World', Medical History Supplement (10), pp 1–13.

Jones, P., F. Hillier and D. Turner (1994). 'Back Street to Side Street to High Street: The Changing Geography of Betting Shops', Geography 79(2), pp 122–8.

Kaplan, S. (1995). 'The Restorative Benefits of Nature: Toward an Integrative Framework', Journal of Environmental Psychology 15(3), pp 169–82.

Karakusevic, P., M. Althorpe and A. Batchelor (2021). Public Housing Works. London: Lund Humphries.

Keizer, K., S. Lindenberg and L. Steg (2008). 'The Spreading of Disorder', Science 322, pp 1681–5.

Keyes, C.L.M. (2002). 'The Mental Health Continuum: From Languishing to Flourishing in Life', Journal of Health and Behaviour Research 43(2), pp 207–22.

Korpela, K.M. (1989). 'Place-identity as a Product of Environmental Self-regulation', Journal of Environment Psychology 9, pp 241–56.

Laaidi, K., A. Zeghnoun, B. Dousset, P. Bretin, S. Vandentorren, E. Giraudet, et al. (2012). 'The Impact of Heat

Islands on Mortality in Paris during the August 2003 Heat Wave', *Environmental Health Perspectives* 120(2), pp 254–9.

Lachowycz, K. and A.P. Jones (2011). 'Greenspace and Obesity: A Systematic Review of the Evidence', *Obesity Reviews* 12(5), pp e183–e9.

Lake, A.A. and T.G. Townshend (2006). 'Obesogenic Environments: Exploring the Built and Food Environments', *Journal of the Royal Society for the Promotion of Health* 126(6), pp 262–7.

Lake, A.A., T.G. Townshend and T. Burgoine (2017). 'Obesogenic Environments'. In: J.L. Buttriss, A.A. Welch, J.M. Kearney and S.A. Lanham-New (eds), *Public Health Nutrition, Second Edition*. The Nutrition Society Textbook Series. Oxford: Wiley-Blackwell.

Larson, R.W. (2000). 'Towards a Psychology of Positive Youth Development', *American Psychologist* 55(1), pp 170–83.

Le Corbusier (2008). *Toward an Architecture*. London: Frances Lincoln.

Lee, K.E., K.J.H. Williams, L.D. Sargent, N.S.G. Williams and K.A. Johnson (2015). '40-second Green Roof Views Sustain Attention: The Role of Micro-breaks in Attention Restoration', *Journal of Environmental Psychology* 42, pp 182–9.

Levitt Bernstein (2019). *Why the Government Should End Permitted Development Rights for Office to Residential Conversion*. London: Levitt Bernstein.

Longo, A., W.G. Hutchinson, R.F. Hunter, M.A. Tully and F. Kee (2015). 'Demand Response to Improved Walking Infrastructure: A Study into the Economics of Walking and Health Behaviour Change', *Social Science & Medicine* 143, pp 107–16.

Lowenthal, D. (1985). *The Past is a Foreign Country*. Cambridge: Cambridge University Press.

Lowenthal, D. (2015). *The Past is a Foreign Country Revisited*. Cambridge: Cambridge University Press.

Lynch, K. (1972). *What Time Is This Place?* Cambridge, MA: MIT Press.

McIntyre, N. (2020). 'English Councils Backpedal on Cycling Schemes after Tory Backlash', *The Guardian*, 15 July.

Mackay, A., D.F. Mackay, C.A. Celis-Morales, D.M. Lyall, S.R. Gray, N. Sattar, J.M.R. Gill, J.P. Pell and J.J. Anderson (2019). 'The Association between Driving Time and Unhealthy Lifestyles: A Cross-sectional, General Population Study of 386,493 UK Biobank Participants', *Journal of Public Health* 41(3), pp 527–34.

McNeely, L.F. and L. Wolverton (2008). *Reinventing Knowledge:*

From Alexandria to the Internet. London: W.W. Norton & Co.

Marí-Dell'Olmo, M., A.M. Novoa, L. Camprubí, et al. (2017). 'Housing Policies and Health Inequalities', *International Journal of Health Services* 47(2), pp 207–32.

Marmot, M., J. Allen, P. Goldblatt, T. Boyce, D. McNeish, M. Grady and I. Geddes (2010). *Fair Society, Healthy Lives – The Marmot Review: Strategic Review of Health Inequalities in England Post-2010*. The Marmot Review, https://www.parliament.uk/global assets/documents/fair-society-healthy-lives-full-report.pdf

Marmot, M., J. Allen, T. Boyce, P. Goldblatt and J. Morrison (2020). *Health Equity in England: The Marmot Review 10 Years On*. London: Institute of Health Equity.

Matz, C.J., M. Egyed, R. Hocking, S. Seenundun, N. Charman and N. Edmonds (2019). 'Human Health Effects of Traffic-related Air Pollution (TRAP): A Scoping Review Protocol', *Systematic Reviews* 8(223), https://doi.org/10.1186/s13643-019-1106-5

MHCLG (2015). *Technical Housing Standards – Nationally Described Space Standards*. London: MHCLG.

MHCLG (2020a). *English Housing Survey 2019 to 2020: Headline Report*. London: MHCLG.

MHCLG (2020b). 'Home Ownership, 2018–19'. In:

English Housing Survey. London: MHCLG.

MHCLG (2021). *National Model Design Code*. London: MHCLG.

Mitchell, R. and F. Popham (2008). 'Effect of Exposure to Natural Environment on Health Inequalities: An Observational Population Study', *The Lancet* 372(9650), pp 1655–60.

Miyazaki, Y. and Y. Motohashi (1995). 'Forest Environment and Physiological Response'. In: Y. Agishi and Y. Ohtsuka (eds), *Recent Progress in Medical Balneology and Climatology*. Hokkaido: Hokkaido University.

Monckton, L. and S. Reilly (2018). 'Wellbeing and the Environment: Why Bother?', *Historic England Research* 11, pp 6–17.

Morris, R.E. (2018). 'The Victorian "Change of Air" as Medical and Social Construction', *Journal of Tourism History* 10(1), pp 45–64.

Mumford, L. (1938). *The Culture of Cities*. London: Martin Secker and Warburg Ltd.

Münzel, T., T. Gori, W. Babisch and M. Basner (2014). 'Cardiovascular Effects of Environmental Noise Exposure', *European Heart Journal* 35(13), pp 829–36.

NHS (2019). 'Putting Health into Place Executive Summary', https://www.england.nhs.uk/wp-content/uploads/2019/09/phip-executive-summary.pdf

NHS Digital (2020). 'Statistics on Obesity, Physical Activity and Diet, England', https://digital.nhs.uk/data-and-information/publications/statistical/statistics-on-obesity-physical-activity-and-diet/england-2020.

National Housing Federation (2020). 'Poor Housing Causing Health Problems for Nearly a Third of Brits During Lockdown', https://www.housing.org.uk/news-and-blogs/news/poor-housing-causing-health-problems-for-nearly-a-third-of-brits-during-lockdown/

Nationwide Building Society (2020). 'The Oakfield Story: A Thoughtful Approach to Community Engagement', https://www.nationwide.co.uk/-/assets/nationwidecouk/documents/about/building-a-better-society/18118-oakfield-blueprint-accessible.pdf?rev=9f7fa72209af433eb630a836ac463f9f

Natural England (2015). 'Econets, Landscape & People: Integrating People's Values and Cultural Ecosystem Services into the Design of Ecological Networks and Other Landscape Change Proposals'. Natural England Commissioned Report NECR180. York: Natural England.

Newham Council (2016). *Betting Shops, Crime and Anti-social Behaviour in Newham*. London: Newham Council.

ONS (2020). 'Housing Affordability in England and Wales', https://www.ons.gov.uk/releases/housingaffordabilityinenglandandwales2020

Owen, R. ([1813]1991). *A New View of Society and Other Writings*. Harmondsworth: Penguin Classics.

Owen, R. ([1813]1991). 'Fourth Essay', in *A New View of Society and Other Writings*, p. 152.

Paddon, H., L.J. Thompson, A. Lanceley, U. Menon and H.J. Chatterjee (2013). 'Mixed Methods Evaluation of Well-being Benefits Derived from a Heritage-in-Health Intervention with Hospital Patients', *Arts and Health: An International Journal of Research, Policy and Practice* 6(1), pp 24–58.

Pasanen, T.P., M.P. White, B.W. Wheeler, J.K. Garrett and L.R. Elliott (2019). 'Neighbourhood Blue Space, Health and Wellbeing: The Mediating Role of Different Types of Physical Activity', *Environment International* 131, 105016.

Pendlebury, J. and J. Brown (2021). *Conserving the Historic Environment*. London: Lund Humphries.

Place Alliance/CPRE (2020). *A Housing Design Audit for England*. London: Place Alliance.

Power, A. and K. Smyth (2016). 'Heritage, Health and Place: The Legacies of Community Based Heritage on Social Well-Being', *Health & Place* 39, pp 160–67.

Pretty, J., J. Peacock, M. Sellens and M. Griffin

(2005). 'The Mental and Physical Health Outcomes of Green Exercise', *International Journal of Environmental Health Research* 15(5), pp 319–37.

Priestley, J.B. (1939). *I Have Been Here Before.* London: Samuel French.

Read, S., A. Comas-Herrera and E. Grundy (2020). 'Social Isolation and Memory Decline in Later-life', *The Journals of Gerontology Series B: Psychological Sciences and Social Sciences.* 75(2), pp 367–76.

Reilly, S., C. Nolan and L. Monckton (2018). *Wellbeing and the Historic Environment.* London: Historic England.

Roberts, M. (2007). 'Sharing Space: Urban Design and Social Mixing in Mixed Income New Communities', *Planning Theory and Practice* 8(2), pp 183–204.

Rook, G.A.W., C.L. Raison and C.A. Lowry (2014). 'Microbial "Old Friends", Immunoregulation and Socio-Economic Status', *Clinical and Experimental Immunology* 177(1), pp 1–12.

Roser, M., E. Ortiz-Espina and H. Ritchie (2013). 'Life Expectancy'. Our World in Data (Revised 2019), https://ourworldindata.org/life-expectancy

Rowe, R. (2019). 'Bicester: Healthy Town, Healthy Lives: Bicester Healthy New Town Case Study'. Cherwell District Council, https://www.cherwell.gov.uk/downloads/file/9157/bicester-healthy-new-town-case-study

Ruokolainen, L., L. von Hertzen, N. Fyhrquist, T. Laatikainen, J. Lehtomaki, P. Auvinen, et al. (2015). 'Green Areas Around Homes Reduce Atopic Sensitisation in Children', *Allergy* 70(2), pp 195–202.

Saelens, B.E. and S. Handy (2008). 'Built Environment Correlates of Walking: A Review', *Medicine and Science in Sports and Exercise* 40(7 Suppl), pp s550–66.

Sallis, J.F., R.A. Millstein and J.A. Carlson (2011). 'Community Design for Physical Activity'. In: A.L. Dannenberg, H. Frumkin, and R.J. Jackson (eds), *Making Healthy Places: Designing and Building for Health, Well-being, and Sustainability.* Washington, D.C.: Island Press.

Samuel, R. (1994). *Theatres of Memory.* London: Verso.

Schuch, F.B., D. Vancampfort, S. Rosenbaum, J. Richards, P.B. Ward and B. Stubbs (2016). 'Exercise Improves Physical and Psychological Quality of Life in People with Depression: A Meta-analysis Including the Evaluation of Control Group Response', *Psychiatry Research* 241, pp 47–54.

Science Advisory Council (2019). 'Landscape Quality: A Rapid Review of the Evidence: Review of Evidence on Assessing and Valuing Landscape Quality and its Aesthetic Dimensions', https://assets.publishing.service.gov.uk/government/uploads/system/uploads/attachment_data/file/856739/defra-sac-landscape-quality-review.pdf

Science for Environment Policy (2016). *Links Between Noise and Air Pollution and Socio-economic Status.* In-depth Report 13 produced for the European Commission, DG Environment by Science Communication Unit, UWE, Bristol, http://ec.europa.eu/science-environment-policy

Shelter (2006). *Chance of a Lifetime: The Impact of Bad Housing on Children's Lives.* London: Shelter.

Shelter (2017). *The Impact of Housing Problems on Mental Health.* London: Shelter.

Silverman, L. (2010). *The Social Work of Museums.* London: Routledge.

Simpson, S.J. (2019). 'Living the Greenway: Evaluations Report'. Belfast Connswater Community Green Trust: Contract No. 05.06.

Singer, M. and S. Clair (2003). 'Syndemics and Public Health: Reconceptualizing Disease in Bio-social Context', *Medical Anthropology Quarterly* 17(4), pp 423–41.

Smith, A., H. Mason, P. Berry, J. Thompson and R. Dunford (n.d.). 'The Value of Green Space in Bicester to Local People'. Oxford: Environmental Change Institute, Oxford University.

References

Song, Y., J. Preston and D. Ogilvie, iConnect Consortium (2017). 'New Walking and Cycling Infrastructure and Modal Shift in the UK: A Quasi-Experimental Panel Study', *Transport Research Part A: Policy and Practice* 95, pp 320–33.

Stafford, M., A. McMunn and R. de Vogli (2011). 'Neighbourhood Social Environment and Depressive Symptoms in Mid-life and Beyond', *Ageing and Society* 31(6), pp 893–910.

Statham, J. and E. Chase (2010). *Childhood Well-being: A Brief Overview*. Loughborough: Childhood Wellbeing Research Centre.

Station Master's Community Garden (n.d.). https://www.stationmasters centre.org/home

Stop the Whoppa (2020), https://stopthewoppa. co.uk/

Sustrans (2016). 'Fit for Life Report on Connect2 Programme', https://www.sustrans.org.uk/our-blog/research/all-themes/all/fit-for-life-report-on-connect-2-programme/

Swinburn, B. and G. Egger (2002). 'Preventive Strategies against Weight Gain and Obesity', *Obesity Reviews* 3(4), pp 289–301.

TCPA (2017). *Understanding Garden Villages: An Introductory Guide*. London: TCPA.

Thomas, A., S. Moore, M. Kyrios, G. Bates, D. Meredyth and G. Jessop (2010). 'Problem Gambling Vulnerability: The Interaction between Access, Individual Cognitions and Group Beliefs/Preferences', Swinburne University of Technology/State Government of Victoria, Department of Justice, Melbourne, Australia.

Thompson, C.W., J. Roe, P. Aspinall, R. Mitchell, A. Clow and D. Miller (2012). 'More Green Space is Linked to Less Stress in Deprived Communities: Evidence from Salivary Cortisol Patterns', *Landscape and Urban Planning* 105(3), pp 221–9.

Tiesler, C.M.T., M. Birk, E. Thiering, G. Kohlböck, S. Koletzko, C-P. Bauer, et al. (2013). 'Exposure to Road Traffic Noise and Children's Behavioural Problems and Sleep Disturbance: Results from the GINIplus and LISAplus Studies', *Environmental Research* 123, pp 1–8.

Townshend, T.G. (2016). 'My Haven, My Sanctuary: Learning from Garden Allotments'. In: D. Babalis (ed.), *Approaching the Integrative City: The Dynamics of Urban Space*. Florence: Altralinea Edizioni.

Townshend, T.G. (2017). 'Toxic High Streets', *Journal of Urban Design* 22(2), pp 167–86.

Townshend, T.G. (ed.) (2021). *Urban Design and Human Flourishing: Creating Places that Enable People to Live Healthy and Fulfilling Lives*: Abingdon: Routledge.

Townshend, T.G. and A.A. Lake (2017). 'Obesogenic Environments: Current Evidence of the Built and Food Environments', *Perspectives in Public Health* 137(1), pp 39–42.

Townshend, T.G. and J. Pendlebury (1999). 'Public Participation in the Conservation of Historic Areas: Case-studies from North-east England', *Journal of Urban Design* 4(3), pp 313–31.

Townshend, T.G. and M. Roberts (2013). 'Affordances, Young People, Parks and Alcohol Consumption', *Journal of Urban Design* 18(4), pp 494–516.

Transport for London/ Mayor of London (2017). *Healthy Streets for London: Prioritising Walking, Cycling and Transport to Create a Healthy City*. London: Transport for London.

Tunbridge, J.E. and G.J. Ashworth (1996). *Dissonant Heritage: The Management of the Past as a Resource in Conflict*. Chichester: John Wiley & Sons.

Ulrich, R.S., R.F. Simon, B.D. Losito, E. Fiorito, M.A. Miles and M. Zelson (1991). 'Stress Recovery to Natural and Urban Environments', *Journal of Environmental Psychology* 11, pp 201–30.

Van Renterghem, T., J. Forssén, K. Attenborough, P.J.J. Defrance, M. Hornikx and J. Kang (2013). 'Using Natural Means to Reduce Surface Transport Noise during

Propagation Outdoors', *Applied Acoustics* 92, pp 86–101.

Visit Copenhagen (2021). 'CopenHill: Futuristic, Unparalleled Ski Slope and Recreational Hill on Top of a New Resource Handling Centre', https://www.visitcopenhagen.com/copenhagen/planning/copenhill-gdk1088237

Waterman, A.S. (1993). 'Two Conceptions of Happiness: Contrasts of Personal Expressiveness (Eudaemonia) and Hedonic Enjoyment', *Journal of Personality and Social Psychology* 64(4), pp 678–91.

Wells, J.C. and E.D. Baldwin (2012). 'Historic Preservation, Significance and Age Value: A Comparative Phenomenology of Historic Charleston and the Nearby New-Urbanist Community of l'On', *Journal of Environmental Psychology* 32(4), pp 384–400.

WHO (1946). *Constitution of the World Health Organization*. New York, 22 July.

WHO (1986). Ottawa Charter, https://www.euro.who.int/__data/assets/pdf_file/0004/129532/Ottawa_Charter.pdf

WHO (2009). 'Global Strategy on Diet, Physical Activity and Health', https://www.who.int/dietphysicalactivity/pa/en/

WHO Healthy Cities (2014). 'Healthy Cities: Promoting Health and Equity – Evidence for Local Policy and Practice', https://www.who.int/publications/i/item/9789289050692

Wild West End (2021). 'Vision', http://www.wildwestend.london/vision

Wilkie, S., T. Townshend, E. Thompson and J. Ling (2018). 'Restructuring the Built Environment to Change Adult Health Behaviors: A Scoping Review Integrated with Behavior Change Frameworks', *Cities & Health* 2(2), pp 198–211.

Wilson, E.O. (1984). *Biophilia: The Human Bond with Other Species*. Cambridge, MA: Harvard University Press.

Wilson, W. and C. Barton (2013). 'Overcrowded Housing (England)'. London: House of Commons Library. Contract No.: Command No. HC 1013.

Yates, G. (2015). *Assessing the Individual and Community Impacts of Stalled Spaces-funded Projects in Glasgow*. Glasgow: Glasgow Centre for Population Health.

Index

Note: *italic* page numbers indicate figures; page numbers followed by n. refer to notes.